REVERSIBLE *Amigurumi*

METEOOR BOOKS

Reversible Amigurumi
Crochet Magical Fairies and Tales
Febby Pranajaya (Chibiscraft)

Have you made characters with patterns from this book?
Share your creations on www.amigurumi.com/5300
or on Instagram with #reversibleamigurumi

Fourth print run, February 2026

First published May 2025
Meteoor Books, Antwerp, Belgium
www.meteoorbooks.com
hello@meteoorbooks.com

Images: Febby Pranajaya (Chibiscraft) & Studio-360.be
Printed and bound by Grafistar

ISBN 978-949164-355-2
D/2025/13.531/1

A catalogue record for this book is available from the Royal Library of Belgium.

REVERSIBLE Amigurumi

Febby Pranajaya Chibiscraft

crochet magical fairies and tales

Welcome to a world where stitches tell stories and yarn weaves magic! In this book, I invite you to step into the enchanting realm of fairy tales, where every project holds a touch of wonder and transformation.

I'm Febby, the person behind *Chibiscraft*, a crochet designer with a passion for creating amigurumi that are both fun to make and full of surprises. My favorite challenge is reversible amigurumi. There's something magical about crafting two connected, functional sides that transform — it's like solving a puzzle, where creativity and analytical thinking come together. This process keeps me constantly inspired to try new ideas and push my boundaries.

My journey as a designer took an exciting turn when I joined a competition held by *Amigurumi.com*. Through that experience, I had the chance to connect with wonderful people who encouraged me to bring this book to life.

This book is inspired by the magic of fairy tales, featuring 12 reversible amigurumi patterns (and 1 Prince Charming) that bring these enchanting stories to life. You will meet delicate fairies, graceful princesses, and a mighty mythical dragon.

Whether you're an ambitious beginner or an experienced crocheter, this book is for anyone who loves a fun project and enjoys learning something new. I hope you'll find joy in making these patterns and feel the same excitement I did while designing them. So grab your yarn and hook, and let's bring these fairy tales to life!

Febby

Thank you!

Special thanks to my parents, who always have my back and lovingly care for my children while I'm at work, to my husband, who gives me long-distance support, and to my children, who are my biggest inspiration.

Thanks to my fans for supporting me all this time.

Thanks to my friends in the crochet community, especially Mónica and Rahma, for helping me improve my skills at the start of my crochet journey.

Thanks to Meteoor Books, Joke, Dora, Bruno and all the pattern testers: Adrienn Wéber, Amanda French, Amy Jones, Anna Persson, Annegret Siegert, Ashton Kirkham, Astrid Markman, Barbara Roman, Bianka Karolkiewicz, Caroline Vandier, Dóra Sipos-Járási, Elise Van den Poel, Esther van Veen, Ilonka Ladenius, Iris Dongo, Jill Constantine, Jimena Bouso, Johanneke Kuilder, Karen Celestine Lee, Karina Green, Kristi Randmaa, Leeke Brandsma, Lotte Nørgaard Pedersen, Louisa Wong, Lutgarde van Dijck, Marianne Rosqvist, Mariska Van den Berg, Marjan Peustjens, Marleen Mertens, Nicole Schavemaker, Rebecca Lyon, Serena Chew, Shannon Kishbaugh, Silke Bridgman, Sonia Fox and Natalie van Dalen.

PAGE 20
PAGE 30
PAGE 38
PAGE 44
PAGE 56
PAGE 64 and 74
PAGE 82
PAGE 92
PAGE 101
PAGE 110
PAGE 120
PAGE 130

BASIC MATERIALS

> This book features **three types of reversible amigurumi:**
>
> 1. **Flower Fairies:** The petals are the reversible element.
> 2. **Partially Reversible Designs:** Only part of the doll is reversible, such as the dragon or the witch.
> 3. **Fully Reversible Designs:** The entire doll can be flipped, like the princesses. For fully reversible designs, the process is more challenging compared to the other types. To make the tension slightly looser and facilitate reversibility, it would be advised to size up your hook a little for these designs. I used a hook size 2.25 mm instead of my usual 2.0 mm.

COLORFUL YARN

For every pattern in this book I've listed the materials used to create the design, including the yarn weight used. Don't feel tied to these yarn choices though: any weight of yarn can be used as a substitute, provided you use the right crochet hook accordingly.

When creating reversible amigurumi, the choice of yarn plays a key role in achieving the desired effect. From my experience, a blend of cotton and acrylic yarn strikes the perfect balance, offering just the right amount of elasticity and durability. 100% acrylic yarn is also a great option, providing flexibility and ease of use. While 100% cotton yarn can work, its lower elasticity demands extra attention to tension to ensure the design can be flipped.

The patterns don't give the yarn quantity. The amounts are rather small and will vary according to how loosely or tightly you crochet. You could use the remnants of other projects or start with a new ball of yarn. One or two balls per color is usually enough.

CROCHET HOOKS

Not only yarn, but hooks as well come in different sorts and sizes. Bigger hooks make bigger stitches than smaller ones. It's important to match the right hook size with the right weight of yarn. In the table below you will find the hook size I recommend for each yarn weight. For amigurumi you generally use a hook two or three sizes smaller than the hook size mentioned on your yarn label.

The crochet fabric should be quite tight, without any gaps through which the stuffing can escape. Using a smaller hook makes it easier to achieve this.

Hooks are usually made from aluminum or steel. Metal

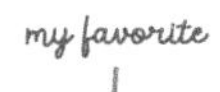

NUMBER (SYMBOL)	1	2	3	4	5	6
CATEGORY NAME	super fine	fine	light	medium	heavy	very heavy
UK YARN TYPE	3 ply	4 ply	double knitting (DK)	aran	chunky	super chunky
US YARN TYPE	Fingering	Sport	Light Worsted	Worsted	Bulky	Extra Bulky
THE HOOK I RECOMMEND IN US SIZE	8 steel to B-1	B-1	B-1 to E-4	E-4 to 7	7 to I-9	I-9 to K-10 1/2
THE HOOK I RECOMMEND IN METRIC SIZE	1.5 to 2.5mm	2.0 to 2.5mm	2.5 to 3.5mm	3.5 to 4.5mm	4.5 to 5.5mm	5.5 to 6.5mm

hooks tend to slip between the stitches more easily. Preferably use a crochet hook with a rubber or ergonomic handle.

STITCH MARKER

A stitch marker is a small clip in metal or plastic. It's a simple tool to mark your starting point and gives you the assurance that you've made the right number of stitches in each round. With your stitch marker, you always mark the last stitch of a round.

STUFFING

For the filling, polyester fiberfill is advised. You can purchase this at any craft shop. It's inexpensive, washable and nonallergenic. Be careful not to overstuff your amigurumi, as the stuffing might stretch the fabric and show through.

FACIAL FEATURES

For some patterns safety eyes are used. These are widely available in craft shops. Be careful when you apply safety eyes: once you put the washer on, you won't be able to pull it off again, so be sure that the post is where you want it to be before attaching the washer.

Alternatively, the features can be embroidered, which is highly recommended if you're making toys for children under the age of three. For embroidery, a tapestry needle with a rounded tip is used.

SAFETY

Please leave out small accessories and wire when the toy is gifted to children under the age of three.

SKILL LEVEL

★ Beginner-friendly / ★★ intermediate / ★★★ advanced

Every pattern is marked with a skill level to indicate how easy it is to make. If this is your first time making reversible amigurumi, it's best to start with a beginner-friendly pattern and work up to the more advanced ones.

PATTERN STRUCTURE

- Unless specifically mentioned, all patterns in this book are worked in **continuous spirals**. Crocheting in spirals can be confusing, since there's no clear indication of where a new round begins and the previous one ends. To keep track of the rounds, you can mark the end of a round with a stitch marker or safety pin. After crocheting the next round, you should end up right above your stitch marker. Move your stitch marker at the end of each round to keep track of where you are.

  At the beginning of each line you will find 'Rnd + a number' to indicate which round you are in. If a round is repeated, you'll read 'Rnd 9 – 12', for example. You then repeat this round four times, crocheting the stitches in rounds 9, 10, 11 and 12.

- Although we usually crochet in rounds, occasionally it happens that we **switch to rows**, going back and forth instead of working in continuous spirals. When we switch to rows, it will be indicated with 'Row + a number'. You end the row with a ch 1 and turn your crochetwork to start the next. Don't count this turning chain as a stitch and skip it when working the next row (unless otherwise mentioned).

- We sometimes work in **joined rounds**, closing the round with a slst in the first stitch and ch 1. When working in joined rounds, we make the first stitch of the next round in the same stitch where we made the slst. Don't count the chain at the beginning and the slst at the end of each round in your stitch total.

- At the end of each line you will find the total number of stitches you should have in **square brackets**, for example [9]. When in doubt, take a moment to check your stitch count.

- When parts of the instructions repeat throughout the round, we place them between **rounded brackets**, followed by the number of times this part should be worked. We do this to shorten the pattern and make it less cluttered.

- When you need to work more than one stitch in the same place, we show this with **a + between the stitches**. For example, "sc + ch-2-picot + sc in next st" means you work a single crochet, a chain-2 picot, and another single crochet — all in the same (next) stitch.

TENSION

It can be challenging to master the tension of your yarn. You're not alone — tension is the one thing that most crocheters have a hard time with. To maintain tension in the working yarn, you may find it helpful to unravel a long end of your yarn ball (your tension is tighter when the weight of the ball pulls your yarn tight), and wrap the yarn around the fingers of the hand opposite the one holding the hook.

When crocheting a doll's hair, you might find the hairpiece is a bit small for the head. The same can happen **when creating a fairy's flower petals**, they might turn out a bit too small to cover your fairy's body. This can happen for a few reasons:

- The head and body are stuffed pieces, and stuffing can cause these to expand, especially if the stitch tension is loose or the piece is slightly overstuffed.
- Yarn thickness can vary between colors, even within the same brand.
- Stitch tension can differ when working in rounds compared to rows.

To avoid this, you can size up your crochet hook a little, to achieve a more relaxed tension.

WRONG AND RIGHT SIDES

To tell the right from the wrong side in crochet:

- The right side has more defined stitches ("V" shapes in single crochet).
- The wrong side shows horizontal bars or loops.
- Check the starting tail: when worked in the round, it's on the wrong side of your work.
- In flat projects the V's at the top of the work are directed towards you on the right side.

AMIGURUMI GALLERY

With each pattern, we have included a URL and QR code that will take you to a dedicated online gallery. Share your finished amigurumi, find inspiration in the color and yarn choices of your fellow crocheters and enjoy the fun of crocheting. Simply follow the link or scan the QR code with your mobile phone. Phones with iOS will scan the QR code automatically in camera mode. For phones with Android you may need to install a QR Reader app first.

Scan or visit
www.amigurumi.com/5300 to share pictures and find inspiration.

STITCHES

If this is your first time making amigurumi, you might find it useful to have a tutorial at hand. With the stitches explained on the following pages you can make all of the amigurumi in this book. We suggest you practice the basic stitches before you start making one of the designs. This will help you to read the patterns and abbreviations more comfortably, without having to browse back to these pages.

→ STITCH TUTORIAL VIDEOS

With each stitch explanation we have included a URL and QR code that will take you to an online stitch tutorial video, showing the technique step by step to help you master it even more quickly. Simply follow the link or scan the QR code with your smartphone. Phones with iOS will scan the QR code automatically in camera mode. For phones with Android you may need to install a QR Reader app first.

INSERT THE HOOK (PLACEMENT OF STITCHES)
With the exception of chains, all crochet stitches require the hook to be inserted in existing stitches. Insert the hook underneath both top loops of the stitch in the row or round below. When inserting the hook, you take it from front to back through a stitch. The point of the hook must always look down or sideways, so the hook doesn't snag the yarn or the fabric.

When asked to crochet FLO / BLO / FP / BP, you make the same stitch, though not in both loops:

Inserting the hook in front loops only (abbreviation: FLO)
When working in Front Loops Only, you pick up only the front loop toward you.
Inserting the hook in back loops only (abbreviation: BLO)
When working in Back Loops Only, you pick up only the back loop away from you.
Inserting the hook around the back post (abbreviation: BP)
The post of the stitch is the main vertical portion of the stitch. Insert the hook from right to left and from back to front to back around the vertical post of the stitch.
Inserting the hook around the front post (abbreviation: FP)
Insert the hook from right to left and from front to back to front around the vertical post of the next stitch.

Scan or visit **www.stitch.show/FLO-BLO** for the video tutorial

Scan or visit **www.stitch.show/BP-FP** for the video tutorial

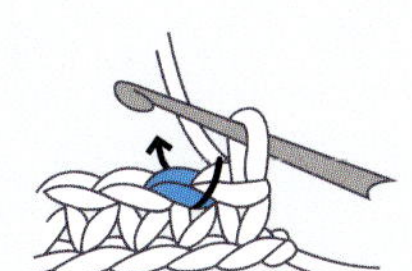
both loops

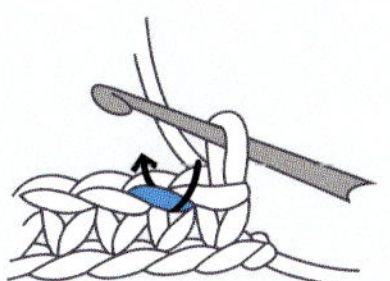
front loops only

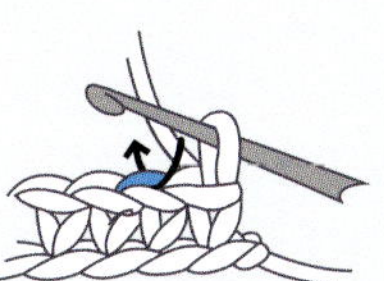
back loops only

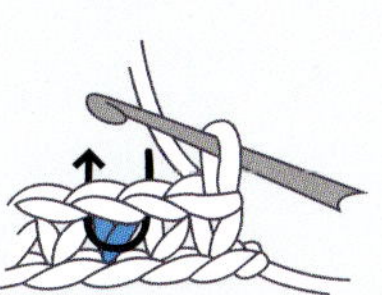
back post

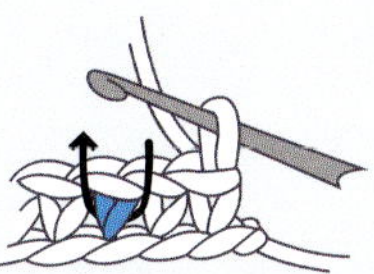
front post

CHAIN (abbreviation: ch)

If you're working in rows, your first row will be a series of chain stitches.

Step 1: Use the hook to draw the yarn through the loop.

Step 2: Pull the loop until tight.

Step 3: Wrap the yarn over the hook from back to front. Pull the hook, carrying the yarn, through the loop already on your hook. You have now completed one chain stitch.

Step 4: Repeat these steps as indicated in the pattern to create a foundation chain.

Scan or visit
www.stitch.show/ch
for the video tutorial

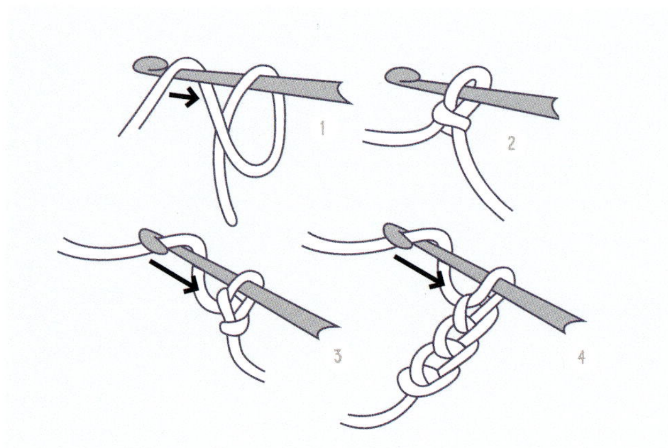

SLIP STITCH (abbreviation: slst)

A slip stitch is used to move across one or more stitches at once or to finish a piece.

Step 1: Insert your hook into the next stitch.

Step 2: Wrap the yarn over the hook and draw through the stitch and loop on your hook at once.

Scan or visit
www.stitch.show/slst
for the video tutorial

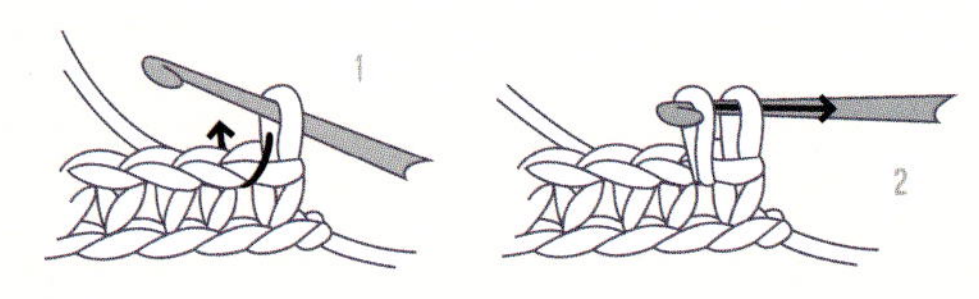

SINGLE CROCHET (abbreviation: sc)

Single crochet is the stitch that will be most frequently used in this book.

Step 1: Insert the hook into the next stitch.

Step 2: Wrap the yarn over the hook. Pull the yarn through the stitch. You will see that there are now two loops on the hook.

Step 3: Wrap the yarn over the hook again and draw it through both loops at once.

Step 4: You have now completed one single crochet.

Step 5: Insert the hook into the next stitch to continue.

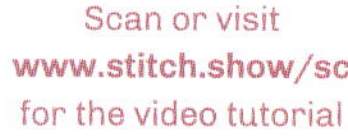

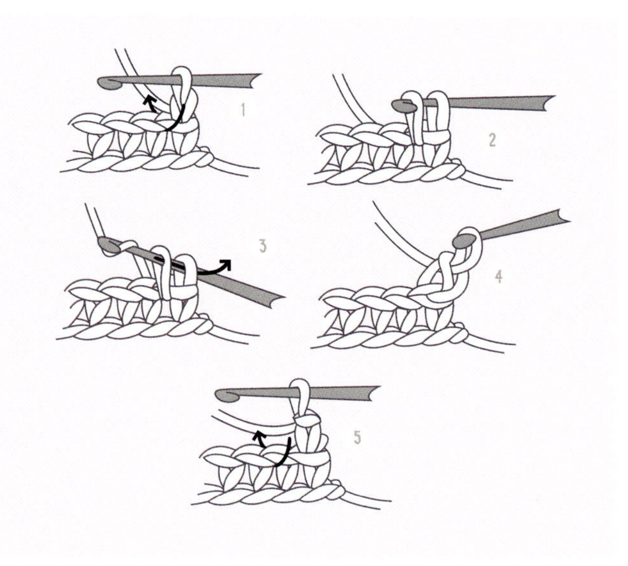

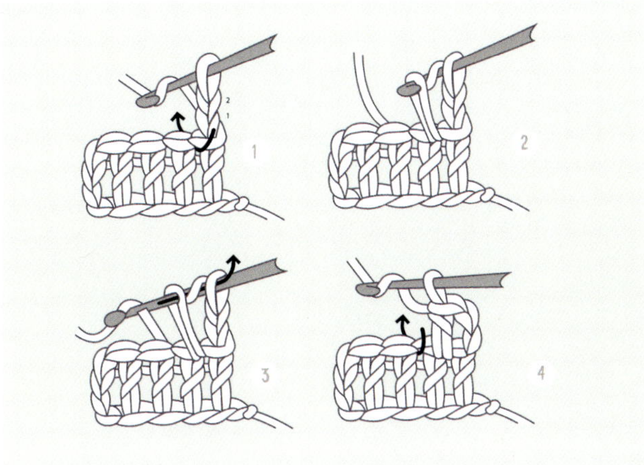

HALF DOUBLE CROCHET

(abbreviation: hdc)

Step 1: Bring your yarn over the hook from back to front before placing the hook in the stitch.

Step 2: Wrap the yarn over the hook and draw the yarn through the stitch. You now have three loops on the hook.

Step 3: Wrap the yarn over the hook again and pull it through all three loops on the hook. You have completed your first half double crochet.

Step 4: To continue, bring your yarn over the hook and insert it in the next stitch.

Scan or visit **www.stitch.show/hdc** for the video tutorial

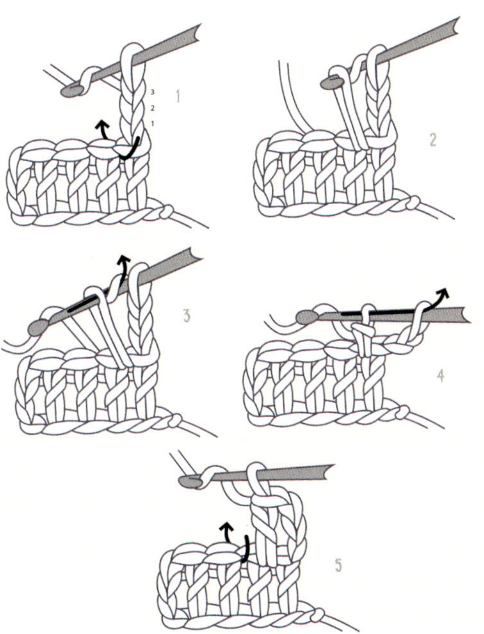

DOUBLE CROCHET (abbreviation: dc)

Step 1: Bring your yarn over the hook from back to front before placing the hook in the stitch.

Step 2: Wrap the yarn over the hook and draw the yarn through the stitch. You now have three loops on the hook.

Step 3: Wrap the yarn over the hook and pull it through the first two loops on the hook. You now have two loops on the hook.

Step 4: Wrap the yarn over the hook one last time and draw it through both loops on the hook. You have now completed one double crochet.

Step 5: To continue, bring your yarn over the hook and insert it in the next stitch.

Scan or visit **www.stitch.show/dc** for the video tutorial

TRIPLE CROCHET (abbreviation: tr)

Step 1: Bring your yarn over the hook twice from back to front before placing the hook in the stitch.
Step 2: Wrap the yarn over the hook and draw the yarn through the stitch. You now have four loops on the hook.
Step 3: Wrap the yarn over the hook again and pull it through the first two loops on the hook. You now have three loops on the hook.
Step 4: Wrap the yarn over the hook again and pull it through the first two loops on the hook. You now have two loops on the hook.
Step 5: Wrap the yarn over the hook again and pull it through the first two loops on the hook. You have now completed one triple crochet. Start the next triple crochet in the next stitch.

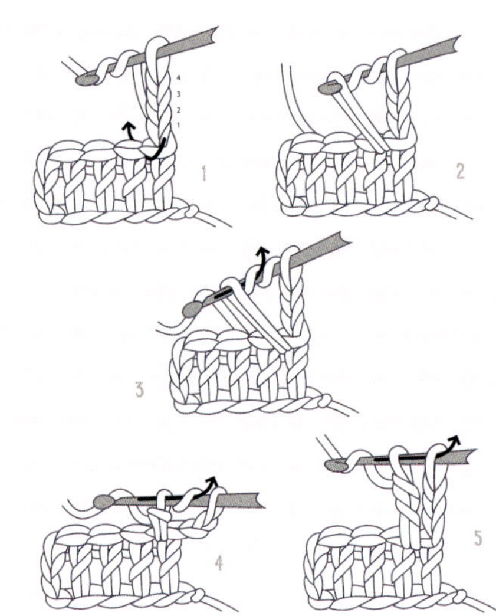

Scan or visit **www.stitch.show/tr** for the video tutorial

DOUBLE TRIPLE CROCHET (abbreviation: dtr)

Step 1: Bring your yarn over the hook three times and insert it in the next stitch.
Step 2: Wrap the yarn over the hook and draw the yarn through the stitch.
Step 3: Wrap the yarn over the hook again and pull it through the first two loops on the hook.
Step 4: Repeat step 3 three more times until you have only one leftover loop on your hook.

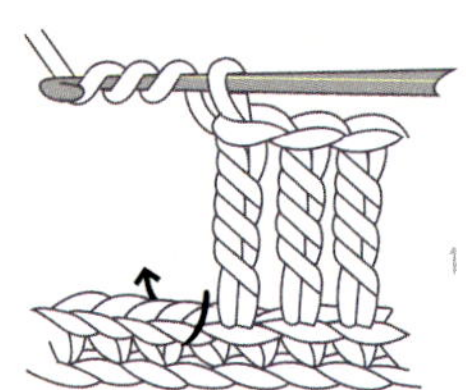

Scan or visit **www.stitch.show/dtr** for the video tutorial

INCREASE (abbreviation: inc)

To increase, two single crochet stitches are made in the same stitch.
Step 1: Make a first single crochet stitch in the next stitch.
Step 2: Make a second single crochet stitch in the same stitch.

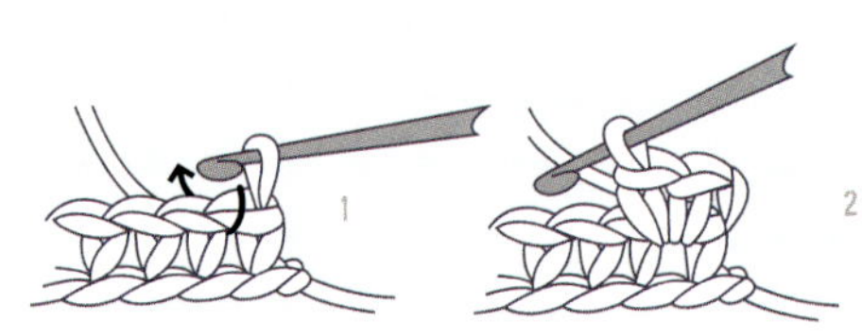

Scan or visit **www.stitch.show/inc** for the video tutorial

You can make an increase with any stitch of your choice. Just make two of the same stitches in one stitch:
hdc increase (hdc inc) – dc increase (dc inc) – tr increase (tr inc) – dtr increase (dtr inc)

Note: A single crochet increase is written as 'inc', without specifically mentioning the single crochet (sc) stitch. When working rounds with various types of increases, the other increases will have a specific mention (like hdc inc, dc inc, or tr inc). When there's no specific mention, you make a single crochet increase.

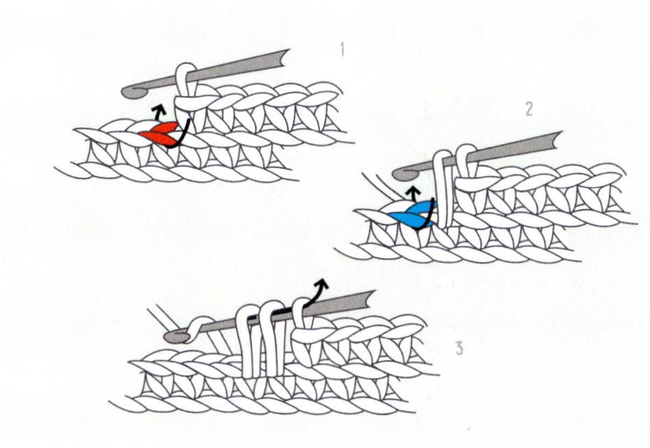

REGULAR DECREASE WORKED THROUGH BOTH LOOPS

(abbreviation: sc2tog)

When two stitches are crocheted together, the number of stitches in a round decreases and the piece shrinks. We use the regular decrease only when explicitly mentioned. For all other instances, the invisible decrease is the preferred option.

Step 1: Insert the hook underneath both loops of your first stitch and pull up a loop.

Step 2: Now insert your hook underneath both loops of the second stitch and pull up a loop. You now have three loops on your hook.

Step 3: Wrap the yarn over the hook and pull it through all three loops on the hook.

Scan or visit **www.stitch.show/sc2tog** for the video tutorial

INVISIBLE DECREASE (abbreviation: dec)

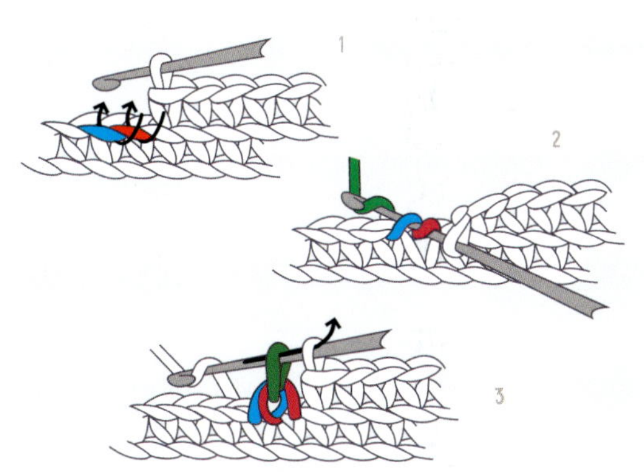

The invisible decrease method will make your decrease stitch look much like the other stitches in the row, resulting in a smooth and even crochet fabric.

Step 1: Insert the hook in the front loop of your first stitch. Now immediately insert your hook in the front loop of the second stitch. You now have three loops on your hook.

Step 2: Wrap the yarn over the hook and pull it through the first two loops on the hook.

Step 3: Wrap the yarn over the hook again and pull it through the remaining two loops on the hook.

Scan or visit **www.stitch.show/dec** for the video tutorial

INVISIBLY DECREASE 3 STITCHES AT ONCE

(abbreviation: sc3tog)

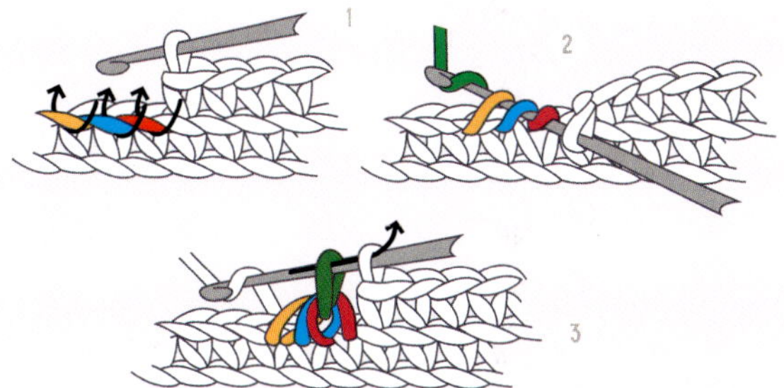

Step 1: Insert the hook under the front loop only of the next three stitches. This gives you four loops on the hook.

Step 2: Wrap the yarn over the hook and pull it through the first three loops on the hook.

Step 3: Wrap the yarn over the hook again and pull it through the remaining two loops on the hook.

Scan or visit **www.stitch.show/sc3tog** for the video tutorial

HALF DOUBLE CROCHET DECREASE

(abbreviation: hdc2tog)

Step 1: Bring your yarn over the hook from back to front before placing the hook in the next stitch. Wrap the yarn over the hook and pull it through the stitch. You now have three loops on your hook.

Step 2: Repeat this from the start in the next stitch. You now have five loops on your hook.

Step 3: Wrap the yarn over your hook once more and pull it through all five loops on your hook.

Note: to make a hdc3tog, work step 1 three times in total, in the three adjacent stitches.

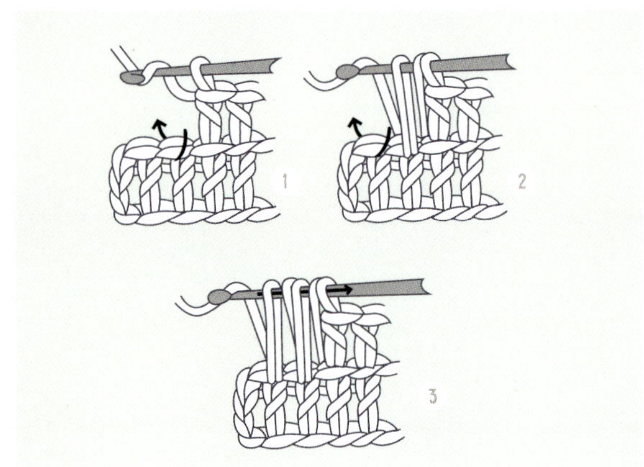

Scan or visit **www.stitch.show/hdcdec** for the video tutorial

DOUBLE CROCHET DECREASE

(abbreviation: dc2tog)

Step 1: Bring your yarn over the hook from back to front before placing the hook in the next stitch. Wrap the yarn over the hook and pull it through the stitch. You now have three loops on the hook. Wrap the yarn over the hook and draw it through the first two loops on the hook. You now have two loops on the hook. Repeat this step from the start in the next stitch. You now have three loops on the hook.

Step 2: Wrap the yarn over the hook once more and pull it through all three loops on the hook.

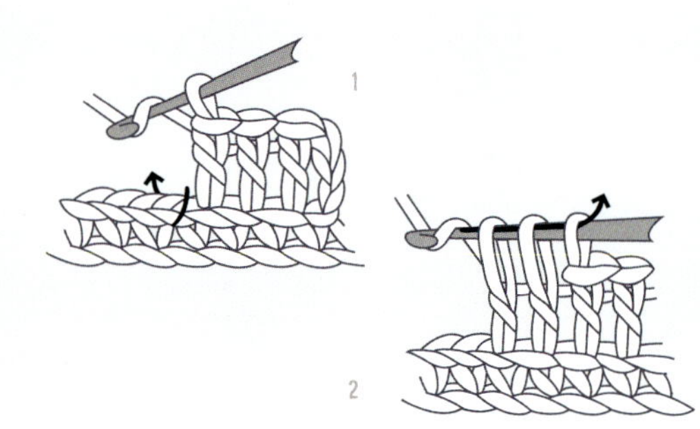

Scan or visit **www.stitch.show/dcdec** for the video tutorial

TRIPLE CROCHET DECREASE

(abbreviation: tr2tog)

Step 1: Bring your yarn over the hook two times from back to front before placing the hook in the next stitch. Wrap the yarn over your hook and pull it through the stitch. You now have four loops on your hook. (Wrap the yarn over your hook and draw it through the first two loops on your hook) repeat 2 times. You now have two loops on your hook. Repeat this step from the start in the next stitch. You now have three loops on your hook.

Step 2: Wrap the yarn over your hook once more and pull it through all three loops on your hook.

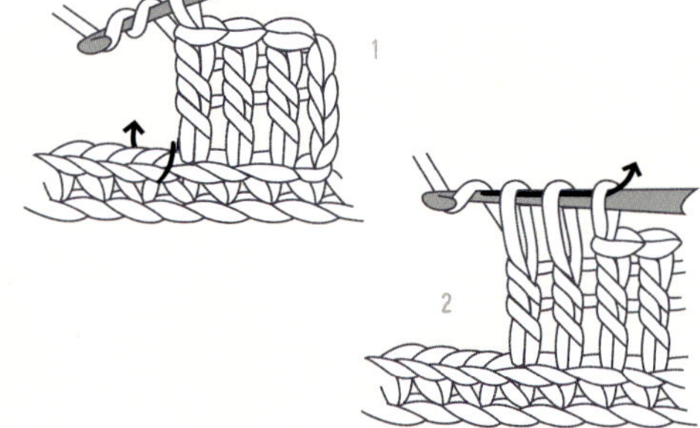

Scan or visit **www.stitch.show/tr2tog** for the video tutorial

Note: to make a tr3tog, work step 1 three times in total, in the three adjacent stitches.

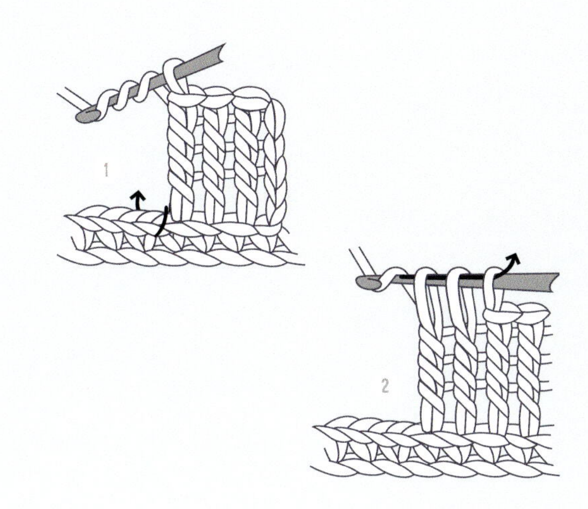

DOUBLE TRIPLE CROCHET DECREASE

(abbreviation: dtr2tog)

Step 1: Bring your yarn over the hook three times from back to front before placing the hook in the next stitch. Wrap the yarn over your hook and pull it through the stitch. You now have five loops on your hook. (Wrap the yarn over your hook and draw it through the first two loops on your hook) repeat 3 times. You now have two loops on your hook. Repeat this step from the start in the next stitch. You now have three loops on your hook.

Step 2: Wrap the yarn over your hook once more and pull it through all three loops on your hook.

Scan or visit **www.stitch.show/dtr2tog** for the video tutorial

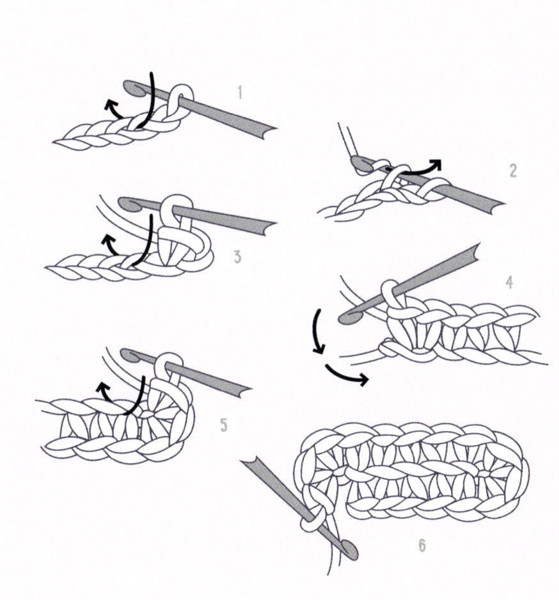

CROCHET AROUND A FOUNDATION CHAIN

Some pieces start with an oval. You make an oval by crocheting around a foundation chain.

Step 1: Crochet a foundation chain with as many chains as mentioned in the pattern and skip the first chain on the hook.

Step 2 – 3: Work a sc stitch in the next chain stitch. Work your crochet stitches into each chain across as mentioned in the pattern.

Step 4: The last stitch before turning is usually an increase stitch.

Step 5: Turn your work upside down to work into the underside of the chain stitches. You'll notice that only one loop is available, simply insert your hook in this loop. Work your stitches into each chain across.

Step 6: When finished, your last stitch should be next to the first stitch you made. You can now continue working in spirals.

Scan or visit **www.stitch.show/oval** for the video tutorial

MAGIC RING

To start an amigurumi piece, you need a little circle. A magic ring is the ideal way to start crocheting in the round as there will be no hole left in the middle of your starting round. You start by crocheting over an adjustable loop and finally pull the loop tight when you have finished the required number of stitches.

Step 1: Start with the yarn crossed to form a circle.

Step 2: Draw up a loop with your hook, but don't pull it tight.

Step 3: Hold the circle with your middle finger and thumb and wrap the working yarn over your index finger.

Step 4 – 5: Make one chain stitch by wrapping the yarn over the hook and pulling it through the loop on the hook.

Step 6: Now insert your hook into the circle and underneath the tail. Wrap the yarn over the hook and draw up a loop.

Step 7: Keep your hook above the circle and wrap the yarn over the hook again.

Step 8: Pull it through both loops on the hook. You have now completed your first single crochet stitch. Continue to crochet (repeating step 6, 7, 8) until you have the required number of stitches as mentioned in the pattern.

Step 9 – 10: Now grab the yarn tail and pull to draw the center of the ring tightly. You can now begin your second round by crocheting into the first single crochet stitch of the magic ring. You can use a stitch marker to remember where you started.

Scan or visit **www.stitch.show/magicring** for the video tutorial

STARTING A CIRCULAR PIECE WITH 2 CHAIN STITCHES

If you don't want to use the magic ring technique, there's an easier way to start crocheting in the round. The downside of this technique is a tiny hole that remains visible in the center of the piece.

Step 1: Start by making a slip knot. Then, make 2 chain stitches and work x sc into the second chain from the hook – where x is the number of sc stitches you would make in your magic ring.

Step 2: Make a slst in the first stitch. You now have a little circle to start with.

Scan or visit **www.stitch.show/2ch** for the video tutorial

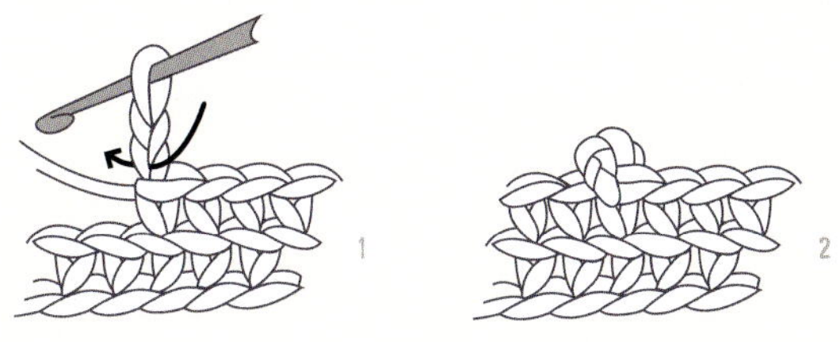

PICOT STITCH (abbreviation: ch-2-picot)

Step 1: Make two chain stitches. Insert your hook in the first chain stitch you made.

Step 2: Wrap the yarn around your hook and draw it through both loops on the hook. You have now completed one picot stitch.

Scan or visit **www.stitch.show/picot** for the video tutorial

BOBBLE STITCH (abbreviation: 3-dc-bobble)

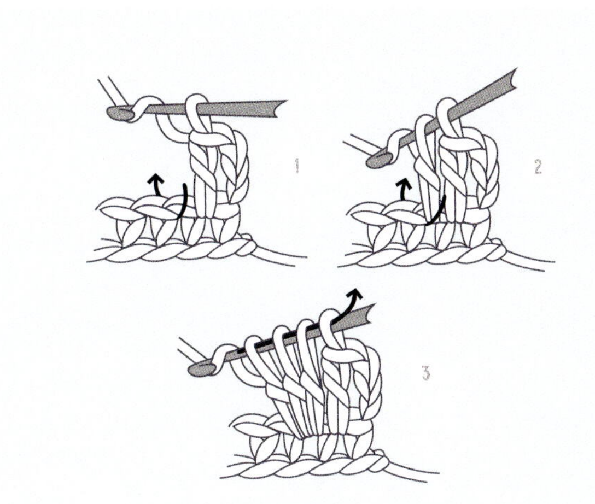

The bobble stitch creates a soft dimensional bobble. Think of it as a cluster of dc stitches worked in the same stitch.

Step 1: Bring your yarn over the hook from back to front before placing the hook in the stitch.

Step 2: Wrap the yarn over the hook and draw the yarn through the stitch. You now have three loops on the hook. Wrap the yarn over the hook again and pull it through the first two loops on the hook. One half-closed double crochet is complete, and two loops remain on the hook.

Step 3: In the same stitch, repeat the preceding steps twice. You should have four loops on your hook. Wrap the yarn over your hook and draw the yarn through all loops on the hook.

Scan or visit **www.stitch.show/bobble** for the video tutorial

INVISIBLE COLOR CHANGE CUT-AND-TIE TECHNIQUE

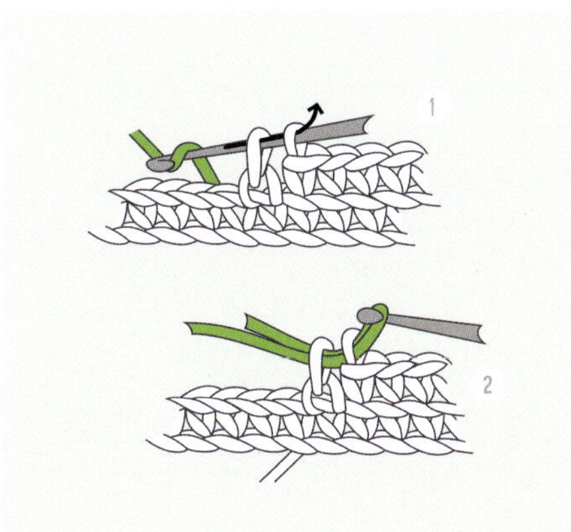

When you want to switch from one color to the next, you work to within two stitches before a color change.

Step 1: Make the next stitch as usual, but don't pull the final loop through.

Step 2: Instead, wrap the new color of yarn around your hook and pull it through the remaining loops. Continue working the next stitch with the new color of yarn. Cut off the non-working yarn and knot the working yarn to the leftover tail. Tie the loose tails in a knot and leave them on the inside.

Note: It's a bit time-consuming, but limits tension issues or colors popping through!

Scan or visit **www.stitch.show/colorchange** for the video tutorial

Scan or visit **www.stitch.show/jacquard** for the video tutorial

COLOR CHANGE JACQUARD

When working jacquard, you work with two colors and leave the yarn you don't use on the back (inside) of the work. When it's time to use it again, you pick up the yarn and carry it across the back (inside) of your work before making the next color change. Take into account that a color change always starts a stitch before. The strands that remain inside your crochetwork between color changes must be loose enough so that the fabric doesn't pucker.

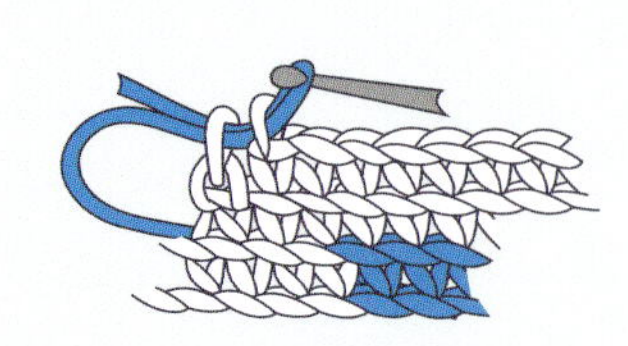

Scan or visit **www.stitch.show/fastenoff** for the video tutorial

FASTENING OFF

Step 1: When you've finished crocheting, cut the yarn a couple of inches / cm from your last stitch. Pull the yarn through the last loop until it is all the way through. You now have a finished knot.

Step 2: Thread the long tail through a tapestry needle and insert it through the back loop of the next stitch. This way the finishing knot will remain invisible in your finished piece. You can use this yarn tail to continue sewing the pieces together.

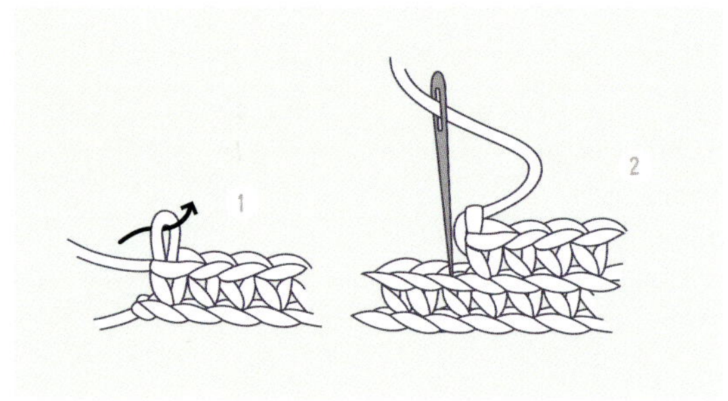

Scan or visit **www.stitch.show/fastenoff-invisible** for the video tutorial

FASTENING OFF INVISIBLE JOIN

Step 1: After completing the last stitch, cut your yarn, leaving a length of 5"/12 cm. Pull the yarn tail all the way through the stitch.

Step 2: Take the yarn tail on your tapestry needle. Insert your needle underneath both loops of the second stitch of the round, from front to back.

Step 3: Then insert it into the back loop only of the last stitch you made. Pull the tail to the back of the work and weave in the yarn end. You will see that your invisible join covers the first stitch of the round.

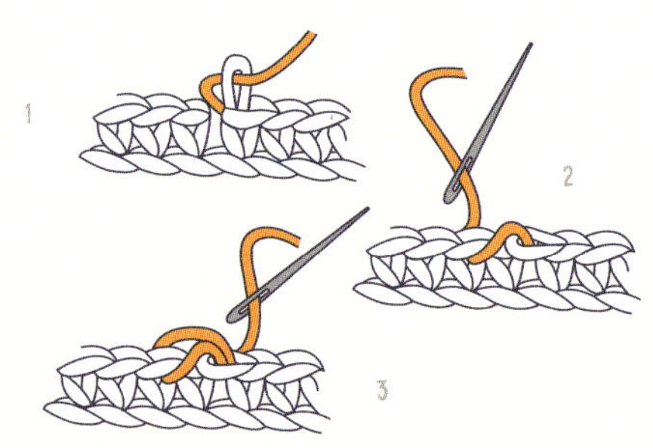

Scan or visit **www.stitch.show/closing** for the video tutorial

CLOSING OFF A PIECE

Step 1: After several decreases in the last round, a small hole will remain at the end of some pieces.

Step 2: Fasten off, leaving a long yarn tail. Thread the yarn tail left at the end of the piece onto a yarn needle, then insert the needle through each of the front loops of the stitches in the last round. Tighten and insert the needle through the nearest stitch, make a knot, and hide the yarn tail inside the piece.

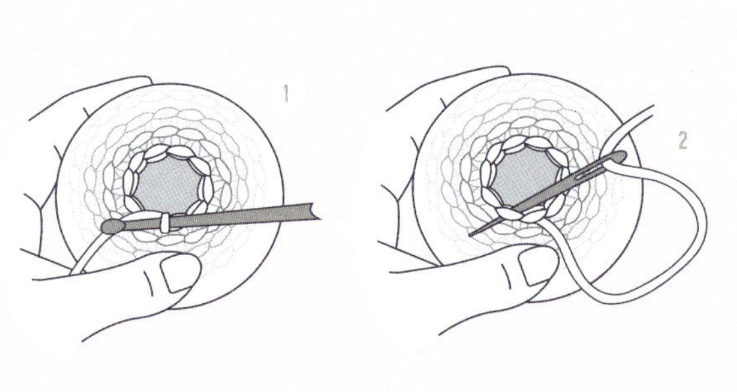

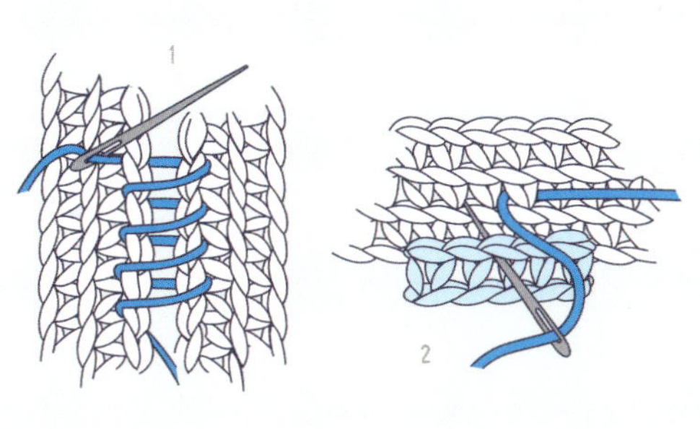

JOINING PARTS SEWING

First, pin the parts you want to sew to one another, so you can evaluate the result and adjust if necessary. If possible, use the leftover yarn tail from when you fastened off, or use a new length of the same yarn color of one of the pieces that you want to join.

Option 1 – When the different pieces are open: position the piece on the body and sew all around it, going through the stitches of both pieces.

Option 2 – When the opening of the different pieces is sewn closed before attaching them to the body: line up the stitches and sew through both loops of the open side and between the stitches of the closed side. Use the same color of yarn as the pieces you want to join together.

TIP: Always make sure the pieces are securely attached so that they can't be pulled off. Make small, neat stitches and try to make them show as little as possible.

Scan or visit **www.stitch.show/joining-sewing** for the video tutorial

EMBELLISHMENT: FRENCH KNOT

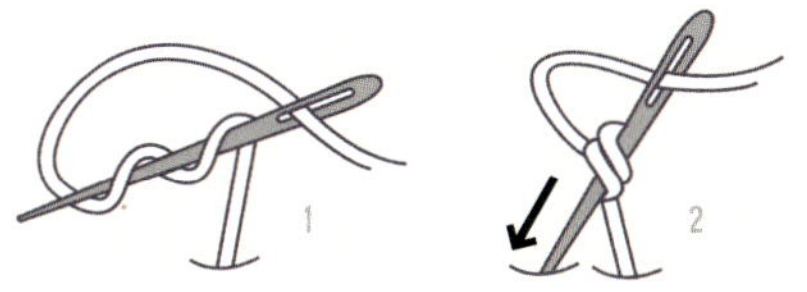

Step 1: Insert the tapestry needle from the back to the front through the stitch where you want the knot to show. Keep the tip of the needle flat against your crochetwork and wrap the yarn around your needle twice.

Step 2: Carefully pull the needle through these loops so that you end up with a double knot. Insert the needle in the crochet stitch next to the knot – not in the same stitch, as this will make the knot disappear – and fasten at the back.

Scan or visit **www.stitch.show/frenchknot** for the video tutorial

EMBELLISHMENT: SURFACE SLIP STITCH

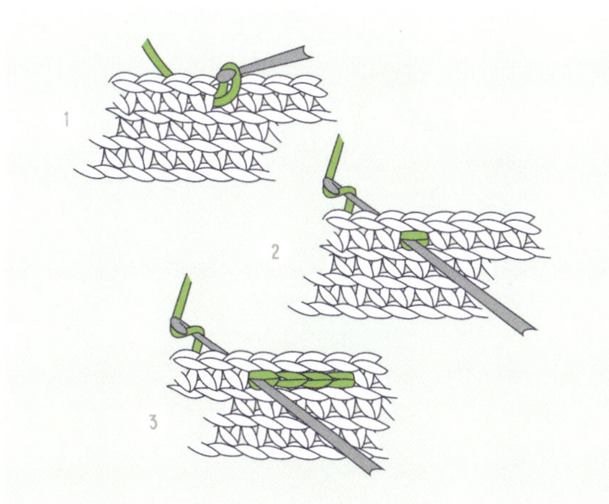

The surface slip stitch is an embellishment of slip stitches worked on top of the fabric of your crochetwork.

Step 1: Insert the hook from the right side to the wrong side where you want your line of slip stitches to start, now wrap the yarn over the hook and draw it through the stitch.

Step 2: Insert the hook in the next stitch, wrap the yarn over the hook. Pull it through the stitch and the loop on the hook. This is the start of your line of surface slip stitches.

Step 3: Repeat this to the end of your crochetwork or in any shape you like.

Scan or visit **www.stitch.show/surfaceslst** for the video tutorial

REVERSIBLE **PRINCESS & FROG**

SKILL LEVEL

★☆☆

SIZE

4.5" / 12 cm tall (princess side) or 2.75" / 7 cm tall (frog side) when made with the indicated yarn.

MATERIALS

- Sport weight yarn in:
  - light peach
  - green
  - pale green
  - pink
  - light pink
  - dark brown
  - gold
  - black (leftover)
  - white (leftover)
- B-1 / 2.25 mm crochet hook
- Yarn needle
- Embroidery needle
- Stitch markers
- Scissors
- Fiberfill for stuffing

Scan or visit www.amigurumi.com/5301 to share pictures and find inspiration.

***Note:** For this type of reversible amigurumi, it's recommended to crochet the stitches a bit more loosely. I use a 2.25 mm crochet hook here instead of a 2 mm crochet hook. By sizing up my crochet hook, I can achieve a more relaxed tension, making it easier to flip the characters at the end.*

PRINCESS

HEAD

→ *in light peach yarn*

Rnd 1: start 6 sc in a magic ring [6]
Rnd 2: inc in all 6 st [12]
Rnd 3: (sc in next st, inc in next st) repeat 6 times [18]
Rnd 4: (sc in next st, inc in next st, sc in next st) repeat 6 times [24]
Rnd 5: (sc in next 3 st, inc in next st) repeat 6 times [30]
Rnd 6 – 8: sc in all 30 st [30]
Rnd 9: (sc in next 9 st, inc in next st) repeat 3 times [33]
Rnd 10 – 14: sc in all 33 st [33]
Rnd 15: (sc in next 9 st, dec) repeat 3 times [30]
Rnd 16: (sc in next 3 st, dec) repeat 6 times [24]
Rnd 17: (sc in next 2 st, dec) repeat 6 times [18]
Rnd 18: (sc in next st, dec) repeat 6 times [12]
Stuff the head firmly with fiberfill.
Rnd 19: BLO dec 6 times [6]
Fasten off, leaving a yarn tail. Using your yarn needle, weave the yarn tail through the front loop of each remaining stitch and pull it tight to close. Weave in the yarn end.

- Using dark brown yarn, embroider the eyes, 2 stitches wide, on round 12. The distance between the eyes should be 5 stitches.
- Split the dark brown yarn in strands and use a single strand to embroider tiny eyelashes on round 12.
- Use a single dark brown strand to embroider eyebrows, 3 stitches wide, on round 9.
- With pink yarn, embroider rosy cheeks between rounds 12-13.
- Split your pink yarn in strands and use a single strand to embroider a smile on round 13. ❶

BODY

start in light peach yarn

Hold the head upside down. Pull up a loop of light peach yarn in the second front loop left on round 18 ❷. Work the first stitch in the same stitch where you attached the yarn.
Rnd 19: ch 1, FLO (sc in next st, inc in next st) repeat 6 times [18]

Rnd 20: (sc in next 5 st, inc in next st) repeat 3 times [21]
Change to pale green yarn.
Rnd 21 – 22: sc in all 21 st [21]
Rnd 23: (sc in next 6 st, inc in next st) repeat 3 times [24]
Fasten off with an invisible join, leaving a long tail for sewing 3.

ARM

→ *make 2, start in light pink yarn*

Rnd 1: start 5 sc in a magic ring [5]
Rnd 2 – 5: sc in all 5 st [5]
Change to light peach yarn.
Rnd 6: sc in all 5 st [5]
Rnd 7: FPsc in next 2 st, sc in next 3 st [5]
Rnd 8 – 11: sc in all 5 st [5]
Fasten off, leaving a long tail for sewing 4.
The arms don't need to be stuffed.

HAIR

→ *in dark brown yarn*

Rnd 1: start 6 sc in a magic ring [6]
Rnd 2: inc in all 6 st [12]
Rnd 3: (sc in next st, inc in next st) repeat 6 times [18]
Rnd 4: (sc in next st, inc in next st, sc in next st) repeat 6 times [24]
Rnd 5: (sc in next 3 st, inc in next st) repeat 6 times [30]
Rnd 6: (sc in next 2 st, inc in next st, sc in next 2 st) repeat 6 times [36]
Rnd 7 – 10: sc in all 36 st [36]
Rnd 11: slst in next 12 st, continue making the hair strands,
Strand 1: ch 17, start in second ch from hook, sc in next 14 ch, hdc in next ch, dc inc in next ch,
Continue on the hair base, skip next 2 st, slst in next st,
Strand 2: ch 9, start in second ch from hook, sc in next 5 ch, hdc in next ch, dc in next ch, 3 tr in next ch,
Continue on the hair base, skip next 3 st, slst in next 2 st,
Strand 3: ch 11, start in second ch from hook, sc in next 5 ch, hdc in next ch, dc in next ch, tr3tog,
Continue on the hair base, skip next 3 st, slst in next st,
Strand 4: ch 20, start in second ch from hook, sc in next 17 ch, slst in next 2 ch,
Continue on the hair base, slst in next st, slst in next 11 st [28 + 4 strands]
Fasten off, leaving a long tail for sewing.
Flip the hair base inside out, so that the wrong side is facing outward. Hide the starting yarn tail on the inside by passing it through the magic ring 5 6.

HAIR BUN

→ *in dark brown yarn*

Rnd 1: start 6 sc in a magic ring [6]
Rnd 2: inc in all 6 st [12]
Rnd 3: (sc in next st, inc in next st) repeat 6 times [18]
Rnd 4: (sc in next st, inc in next st, sc in next st) repeat 6 times [24]
Rnd 5 – 6: sc in all 24 st [24]
Rnd 7: (sc in next 6 st, dec) repeat 3 times [21]
Fasten off with an invisible join, leaving a long tail for sewing.
Flip the hair bun inside out, so that the wrong side is

1
2
3
4
5
6
7
8
9
10
11
12
13
14
15
16

facing outward. Hide the starting yarn tail on the inside by passing it through the magic ring.

SKIRT

→ in pale green yarn

Leave a 4" / 10 cm long starting yarn tail, this will later be used to join the princess and the frog together.
Rnd 1: start 6 sc in a magic ring [6]
Rnd 2: inc in all 6 st [12]
Rnd 3: (sc in next st, inc in next st) repeat 6 times [18]
Rnd 4: (sc in next st, inc in next st, sc in next st) repeat 6 times [24]
Rnd 5: (sc in next 3 st, inc in next st) repeat 6 times [30]
Rnd 6: (sc in next 2 st, inc in next st, sc in next 2 st) repeat 6 times [36]
Rnd 7: (sc in next 5 st, inc in next st) repeat 6 times [42]
Rnd 8: (sc in next 3 st, inc in next st, sc in next 3 st) repeat 6 times [48]
Rnd 9 – 10: sc in all 48 st [48]
Rnd 11: (sc in next 7 st, inc in next st) repeat 6 times [54]
Rnd 12 – 16: sc in all 54 st [54]
Rnd 17: (sc in next 4 st, inc in next st, sc in next 4 st) repeat 6 times [60]
Rnd 18 – 21: sc in all 60 st [60]
Change to light pink yarn. Don't fasten off the pale green yarn, but bring the yarn to the outside.
Rnd 22 – 23: BLO sc in all 60 st [60]
Rnd 24: (sc in next 9 st, inc in next st) repeat 6 times [66]
Rnd 25 – 26: sc in all 66 st [66]
Fasten off with an invisible join and weave in the yarn end.

Make frills in the front loops left on round 21. Hold the skirt with the open side downward. Insert your hook in the first front loop and pull up a loop of the pale green yarn ⑦.
Round of frills: work this round in FLO, skip the first st (where you pulled up a loop of the pale green yarn), sc in next st, hdc in next 3 st, sc in next st, (slst in next st, sc in next st, hdc in next 3 st, sc in next st) repeat 9 times [59] ⑧
Slst in next st. Fasten off and weave in the yarn end.

Hold the skirt with the open side upward. Pull up a loop of light pink yarn in the first front loop left on round 22 ⑨. Work the first stitch in the same stitch where you attached the yarn. Work in joined rounds.
Rnd 23: work this round in FLO, ch 2, dc in next 4 st, dc inc in next st, (dc in next 4 st, dc inc in next st) repeat 11 times, slst in first st [72]
Rnd 24: ch 2, dc in next 5 st, dc inc in next st, (dc in next 5 st, dc inc in next st) repeat 11 times, slst in first st [84]
Change to pink yarn.
Rnd 25: ch 1, sc in all 84 st, slst in first st [84]
Fasten off and weave in the yarn end.

With pink yarn, make a French knot in every slst of the pale green frills ⑩.

TIARA ⑪

→ in gold yarn

Ch 6. Crochet in rows.
Row 1: start in second ch from hook, slst in this ch, ch 2, slst in next ch on the foundation chain, sc +

ch-2-picot + sc in next ch, slst in next ch, ch 2, slst in next ch on the foundation chain [7]
Fasten off, leaving a long tail for sewing (12).

GOLDEN BALL

→ *in gold yarn*

Rnd 1: start 6 sc in a magic ring [6]
Rnd 2: inc in all 6 st [12]
Rnd 3: (sc in next 3 st, inc in next st) repeat 3 times [15]
Rnd 4 – 5: sc in all 15 st [15]
Rnd 6: (sc in next 3 st, dec) repeat 3 times [12]
Stuff the ball lightly with fiberfill.
Rnd 7: dec 6 times [6]
Fasten off, leaving a long tail for sewing. Using your yarn needle, weave the yarn tail through the front loop of each remaining stitch and pull it tight to close. Leave a long tail for sewing (13).

ASSEMBLY

- Flatten the opening of the arms and sew them to the body, between rounds 19 and 20.
- Position the hair base on the head. The distance between the hair base at the back of the head and the body should be 3 rounds. Make sure that the bangs are parted in the middle of the face. Sew the last round of the hair base to the head.
- Position the first hair strand to the right, with the wrong side facing outward. Sew it just below the hair base, at round 13 of the head, and leave the tip unsewn.
- Position the fourth hair strand to the left, with the right side facing outward. Sew it just below the hair base, at round 13 of the head, and leave the tip unsewn.
- Position the second hair strand to the right and the third hair strand to the left. Sew the tip of strand 2 on strand 1, and the tip of strand 3 on strand 4.
- Sew the hair bun on top of the hair base. Stuff the bun with fiberfill before closing the seam.
- Sew the tiara in front of the hair bun, with the wrong side facing forward (14) (15).
- Sew the body to the skirt, between rounds 4-5 of the skirt. Stuff the body with fiberfill before closing the seam.
- Pin and sew the golden ball to the body and both hands (16).

FROG

BODY

→ *in green yarn*

Leave a 4" / 10 cm long starting yarn tail, this will later be used to join the princess and the frog together.
Rnd 1: start 6 sc in a magic ring [6]
Rnd 2: inc in all 6 st [12]
Rnd 3: (sc in next st, inc in next st) repeat 6 times [18]
Rnd 4: (sc in next st, inc in next st, sc in next st) repeat 6 times [24]
Rnd 5: (sc in next 3 st, inc in next st) repeat 6 times [30]
Rnd 6: (sc in next 2 st, inc in next st, sc in next 2 st) repeat 6 times [36]
Rnd 7: (sc in next 5 st, inc in next st) repeat 6 times [42]
Rnd 8: (sc in next 3 st, inc in next st, sc in next 3 st) repeat 6 times [48]
Rnd 9 – 10: sc in all 48 st [48]
Rnd 11: (sc in next 7 st, inc in next st) repeat 6 times [54]

17
18
19
20
21
22
23
24
25
26
27
28
29
30
31

Rnd 12 – 16: sc in all 54 st [54]
Rnd 17: (sc in next 4 st, inc in next st, sc in next 4 st) repeat 6 times [60]
Rnd 18 – 23: sc in all 60 st [60]
Rnd 24: (sc in next 9 st, inc in next st) repeat 6 times [66]
Rnd 25 – 26: sc in all 66 st [66]
Fasten off with an invisible join, leaving a 20" / 50 cm long yarn tail (17). This will later be used to sew the princess and the frog together.

FRONT LEG

→ *make 2, in green yarn*

Rnd 1: start 6 sc in a magic ring [6]
Rnd 2: inc in all 6 st [12]
Rnd 3 – 4: sc in all 12 st [12]
Rnd 5: (sc in next 4 st, dec) repeat 2 times [10]
Rnd 6: (sc in next 3 st, dec) repeat 2 times [8]
Rnd 7: (sc in next 2 st, dec) repeat 2 times [6]
Rnd 8: slst in next st, (ch 3, start in second ch from hook, sc in this ch, slst in next ch, then FLO slst in next st on the front leg) repeat 3 times [3 toes] Leave the remaining stitches unworked.
The front leg doesn't need to be stuffed. Flatten the leg with the toes at the front.
Fasten off, leaving a long tail for sewing (18).

HIND LEG

→ *make 2, in green yarn*

Rnd 1: start 6 sc in a magic ring [6]
Rnd 2: inc in all 6 st [12]
Rnd 3: (sc in next st, inc in next st) repeat 6 times [18]
Rnd 4: (sc in next 8 st, inc in next st) repeat 2 times [20]
Continue making the thigh.
Rnd 5a: sc in next 10 st, mark the next stitch on Rnd 4 with a stitch marker, ch 2 (19), skip 10 st [10] (20)
Rnd 6a: sc in next 10 st, sc in next 2 ch [12] (21)
Rnd 7a: (sc in next 5 st, inc in next st) repeat 2 times [14]
Rnd 8a – 9a: sc in all 14 st [14]
Rnd 10a: (sc in next 5 st, dec) repeat 2 times [12]
Rnd 11a: dec 6 times [6]
Fasten off, leaving a long yarn tail. Using your yarn needle, weave the yarn tail through the front loop of each remaining stitch and pull it tight to close. Leave a long tail for sewing (22). Stuff the thigh lightly with fiberfill.
Continue making the lower leg. Hold the leg with the magic ring facing you and pull up a new loop of green yarn in the marked stitch on round 4 (23). Work the first stitch in the same stitch where you attached the yarn.
Rnd 5b: ch 1, sc in next 2 st, dec, sc in next 3 st, dec, sc in next st, sc in the other side of next 2 ch [10] (24)
Rnd 6b – 7b: sc in all 10 st [10]

Rnd 8b: (sc in next 3 st, dec) repeat 2 times [8]
Rnd 9b: sc in all 8 st [8]
Stuff the lower leg lightly with fiberfill and continue stuffing as you go.
Rnd 10b: (sc in next 2 st, dec) repeat 2 times [6]
Rnd 11b: slst in next 3 st, (ch 3, start in second ch from hook, sc in this ch, slst in next ch, FLO slst in next st on the lower leg) repeat 3 times [3 toes]
Fasten off, leaving a long tail for sewing 25.

BELLY

→ *in pale green yarn*

Crochet in rows.
Row 1: start in a magic ring: sc, 2 hdc, sc, ch 1, turn [4]
Tighten the magic ring, but don't join.
Row 2: inc in next st, hdc inc in next 2 st, inc in next st, ch 1, turn [8]
Row 3: sc in next st, inc in next st, (hdc in next st, hdc inc in next st) repeat 2 times, sc in next st, inc in next st, ch 1, turn [12]
Row 4: sc in next st, inc in next st, sc in next st, (hdc in next st, hdc inc in next st, hdc in next st) repeat 2 times, sc in next st, inc in next st, sc in next st, ch 1, turn [16]
Row 5: sc in next 3 st, inc in next st, (hdc in next 3 st, hdc inc in next st) repeat 2 times, sc in next 3 st, inc in next st, ch 1, turn [20]
Row 6: sc in next 2 st, inc in next st, sc in next 2 st, (hdc in next 2 st, hdc inc in next st, hdc in next 2 st) repeat 2 times, sc in next 2 st, inc in next st, sc in next 2 st [24]
Don't turn. Continue working in the row-ends along the straight edge 26.
Row 7: ch 1, sc in next 11 row-ends, slst in first st of Row 6 [12]
Fasten off, leaving a long tail for sewing 27.

EYE

→ *make 2, start in black yarn*

Rnd 1: start 6 sc in a magic ring [6]
Rnd 2: inc in all 6 st, slst in first st [12]
Change to green yarn. The next stitch is the new beginning of the round.
Tip: *Work the slst in the next round rather loosely, so it's not too hard to work into them in round 4.*
Rnd 3: BLO slst in all 12 st [12]
Rnd 4: BLO sc in next 10 st, ch 1, turn [10] Leave the remaining stitches unworked.
Continue crocheting in rows.
Row 5: (sc in next 3 st, dec) repeat 2 times, ch 1, turn [8]
Row 6: dec 4 times, slst in first st [4]
Fasten off, leaving a long tail for sewing.
You can stuff the eye lightly with fiberfill, but stuffing is optional 28.

Hold the eye with the black part facing you. Pull up a loop of green yarn in the front loop of the first unworked stitch of round 3 29. Skip the stitch where you attached the yarn and work in the green front loops left on Rnd 3.
Eyelid round: work this round in FLO, slst in next st, sc in next 8 st, slst in next st [10]
Fasten off and weave in the yarn ends 30.

CHEEK

→ *make 2, in pink yarn*

Rnd 1: start 7 sc in a magic ring [7]
Slst in next st. Fasten off, leaving a long tail for sewing.

32

33

34

CROWN

→ *in gold yarn*

Leave a long starting yarn tail for sewing. Ch 16.
Rnd 1: start in second ch from hook, sc in all 15 ch, slst in first st to make a circle, ch 1 [15]
Rnd 2: sc in all 15 st [15]
Rnd 3: (slst in next st, sc + ch-2-picot + sc in next st, slst in next st) repeat 5 times [25]
Fasten off and weave in the yarn end.

ASSEMBLY

- Sew the eyes on top of the body, between rounds 7 and 8. The distance between the eyes should be about 11 stitches.
- Sew the belly to the body, covering the last 10 rounds of the body.
- Sew the front legs next to the belly, covering the last 7 rounds of the body.
- Sew the hind legs to the sides of the body, positioning them right next to the front legs. Leave the tops of the hind legs unsewn. Make sure they are sewn on tightly to prevent them from coming loose when the frog is turned inside out.
- Using white yarn, embroider a white flare on the eyes.
- Using black yarn, embroider the mouth on round 8.
- Sew the cheeks between rounds 13-15.
- Sew the crown on top of the head 31.

JOINING THE PRINCESS & FROG

Flip the princess and the frog inside out, so that the wrong sides of both are outward. Make a knot with the yarn tails left from the magic rings. Try to leave a small space between both pieces 32.
Flip the frog back, so the right side is outward. Don't flip the princess back, but keep her with the wrong side outward. The pieces don't need to be stuffed. Gently push the princess inside the frog 33.
With the green yarn tail left on the body of the frog, sew the last rounds of both the frog and the princess together, using only the back loops on both rounds for sewing 34.

REVERSIBLE PEONY FAIRY

SKILL LEVEL

SIZE

4.5" / 12 cm tall when made with the indicated yarn.

MATERIALS

- Sport weight yarn in:
  - coral
  - yellow
  - lime green
  - green
  - light peach
  - dark brown (leftover)
  - peach (leftover)
- B-1 / 2.0 mm crochet hook
- Yarn needle
- Embroidery needle
- Stitch marker
- Fiberfill for stuffing
- Scissors
- Optional: flower wire (gauge #22, 3"/8 cm long)
- Optional: pliers

Scan or visit www.amigurumi.com/5302 to share pictures and find inspiration.

INNER PETAL 1

make 5, in coral yarn

Ch 14. Stitches are worked around both sides of the foundation chain.
Rnd 1: start in second ch from hook, sc in next 12 ch, 3 sc in next ch. Continue on the other side of the foundation chain, sc in next 11 ch, inc in next ch [28]
Rnd 2: inc in next st, sc in next 6 st, hdc in next 5 st, hdc inc in next 3 st, hdc in next 5 st, sc in next 6 st, inc in next 2 st [34]
Rnd 3: sc in next st, inc in next st, sc in next 7 st, hdc in next 4 st, hdc inc in next st, hdc in next st, hdc inc in next 2 st, hdc in next st, hdc inc in next st, hdc in next 4 st, sc in next 7 st, (sc in next st, inc in next st) repeat 2 times [41]
Rnd 4: sc in next 2 st, inc in next st, sc in next 8 st, hdc in next 3 st, (hdc inc in next st, hdc in next st) repeat 2 times, sc in next 2 st, (hdc in next st, hdc inc in next st) repeat 2 times, hdc in next 3 st, sc in next 11 st [43] Leave the remaining stitch unworked.
Fasten off on 4 petals, leaving a 4"/10 cm long tail for sewing. Don't fasten off on the fifth petal. Continue making the upper skirt.

UPPER SKIRT

in coral yarn

Make the upper skirt by joining 5 petals. Crochet 5 sc in each petal. For each you start in the first stitch after the last stitch of round 4. Continue crocheting with the coral yarn from the fifth petal 2.
Rnd 1: (sc in next 5 st) repeat for 5 petals [25] 3 4
Take a moment to weave in the yarn tails of each petal. Thread the yarn tail onto your yarn needle and pull it through to the back of the piece 5.
Note: *Since there are only 4 yarn tails, we'll later use the ending yarn tail to join the last petal to the first.*
Start round 2 by connecting the piece to a circle. Make the first stitch in the fifth petal, count 5 stitches before the connection with the fourth petal. This is where the first stitch of round 2 starts 6.
Rnd 2: (sc in next st, sc2tog, sc in next 2 st, sc2tog) repeat 3 times, sc in next st, sc2tog, sc in next st [18]
Fasten off with an invisible join, leaving a 4"/ 10 cm long tail for sewing. Use this yarn tail to sew up the last and first petal 7.

MIDDLE PETAL

→ *make 5, in coral yarn*

Ch 14. Stitches are worked around both sides of the foundation chain.
Rnd 1: start in second ch from hook, sc in next 12 ch, 3 sc in next ch. Continue on the other side of the foundation chain, sc in next 11 ch, inc in next ch [28]
Rnd 2: inc in next st, sc in next 5 st, hdc in next 3 st, dc in next 3 st, dc inc in next 3 st, dc in next 3 st, hdc in next 3 st, sc in next 5 st, inc in next 2 st [34]
Rnd 3: sc in next st, inc in next st, sc in next 5 st, hdc in next 3 st, dc in next 3 st, dc inc in next st, dc in next st, dc inc in next 2 st, dc in next st, dc inc in next st, dc in next 3 st, hdc in next 3 st, sc in next 5 st, (sc in next st, inc in next st) repeat 2 times [41]
Rnd 4: sc in next 2 st, inc in next st, sc in next 5 st, hdc in next 3 st, dc in next 3 st, (dc inc in next st, dc in next st) repeat 2 times, dc inc in next 2 st, (dc in next st, dc inc in next st) repeat 2 times, dc in next 3 st, hdc in next 3 st, sc in next 7 st [44] Leave the remaining stitch unworked. Fasten off, leaving a 4"/ 10 cm long tail for sewing 8.

OUTER PETAL

→ *make 5, in coral yarn*

Ch 11. Stitches are worked around both sides of the foundation chain.
Rnd 1: start in second ch from hook, sc in next 9 ch, 3 sc in next ch. Continue on the other side of the foundation chain, sc in next 8 ch, inc in next ch [22]
Rnd 2: inc in next st, sc in next 2 st, hdc in next 3 st, dc in next 3 st, dc inc in next 3 st, dc in next 3 st, hdc in next 3 st, sc in next 2 st, inc in next 2 st [28]
Rnd 3: sc in next st, inc in next st, sc in next 2 st, hdc in next 3 st, dc in next 3 st, dc inc in next 6 st, dc in next 3 st, hdc in next 3 st, sc in next 2 st, (sc in next st, inc in next st) repeat 2 times [37]
Rnd 4: sc in next 2 st, inc in next st, sc in next st, hdc in next 3 st, dc in next 3 st, (dc in next st, dc inc in next st) repeat 7 times, dc in next 3 st, hdc in next 3 st, sc in next 3 st [41] Leave the remaining stitch unworked. Fasten off with an invisible join and weave in the yarn ends 9. Mark the stitch in which you made the invisible join with a stitch marker for later reference.

HEAD

→ *start in lime green yarn*

Rnd 1: start 6 sc in a magic ring [6]
Rnd 2: inc in all 6 st [12]
Rnd 3: BLO (sc in next st, inc in next st) repeat 6 times [18]
Change to yellow yarn.
Rnd 4: BLO (sc in next st, inc in next st, sc in next st) repeat 6 times [24]
Rnd 5: (sc in next 3 st, inc in next st) repeat 6 times [30]
Continue working with 2 colors, alternating light peach and yellow yarn. The color change is indicated in italics.
Note: *I use the cut-and-tie technique (p. 17). It's a bit time-consuming, but limits tension issues or colors popping through.*
Rnd 6: *(yellow)* (sc in next 4 st, inc in next st) repeat 2 times, sc in next 3 st, *(light peach)* sc in next st, inc in next st, sc in next 3 st, *(yellow)* sc in next st, inc in next st, (sc in next 4 st, inc in next st) repeat 2 times [36]
Rnd 7: *(yellow)* sc in next 14 st, *(light peach)* sc in next 8 st, *(yellow)* sc in next 14 st [36]
Rnd 8: *(yellow)* sc in next 13 st, *(light peach)* sc in next 10 st, *(yellow)* sc in next 13 st [36]
Rnd 9 – 12: *(yellow)* sc in next 13 st, *(light peach)* sc in next 11 st, *(yellow)* sc in next 12 st [36]

1 2 3 4 5 6 7 8 9

Rnd 13: *(yellow)* (sc in next 4 st, dec) repeat 2 times, sc in next 2 st, *(light peach)* sc in next 2 st, dec, sc in next 4 st, dec, *(yellow)* (sc in next 4 st, dec) repeat 2 times [30]
Rnd 14: *(yellow)* (sc in next 3 st, dec) repeat 2 times, sc in next 2 st, *(light peach)* sc in next st, dec, sc in next 3 st, dec, *(yellow)* (sc in next 3 st, dec) repeat 2 times [24]
Rnd 15: *(yellow)* (sc in next 2 st, dec) repeat 2 times, sc in next 2 st, *(light peach)* dec, sc in next 2 st, dec, *(yellow)* (sc in next 2 st, dec) repeat 2 times [18]
Continue working in yellow yarn.
Rnd 16: (sc in next st, dec) repeat 6 times [12]
Stuff the head firmly with fiberfill.
Rnd 17: BLO dec 6 times [6]
Fasten off, leaving a yarn tail. Using your yarn needle, weave the yarn tail through the front loop of each remaining stitch and pull it tight to close. Weave in the yarn end 10.

FRILLS (STAMENS) ON HEAD

→ *in yellow yarn*

The stamens are worked in the leftover front loops of

rounds 2 and 3 of the head.
Hold the head with the magic ring facing you. Pull up a loop of yellow yarn in the first front loop left on round 2 (11).
Rnd 3 – 4: ch 3, slst in the same stitch where you joined the yarn, (slst + ch 4 + slst in next st, slst + ch 3 + slst in next st) repeat 14 times, slst + ch 4 + slst in next st (12).
Fasten off and weave in the yarn end.

HAIR STRAND

→ *in yellow yarn*

Ch 14. Crochet in rows.
Row 1: start in second ch from hook, slst in this ch, sc in next ch, inc in next 3 ch, sc in next 4 ch, hdc in next 2 ch, dc in next ch, dc inc in next ch [17]
Fasten off, leaving a long tail for sewing (13).

FLOWER HEADBAND

→ *in coral yarn*

Leave a 4"/ 10 cm long starting tail.
Rnd 1: start a magic ring with (ch 3, 2 slst in magic ring) repeat 5 times.
Tighten the magic ring. Fasten off, leaving a 4" / 10 cm long tail to tie the headband (14).

DETAILS OF HAIR & FACE

- Sew the hair strand to the left side of the face (based on the fairy's viewpoint), with the wrong side facing outward.
- Embroider the bangs on the right side of the face using yellow yarn, covering rounds 6-11.
- Embroider the eyes using dark brown yarn, over round 10, about 5 stitches apart.
- Split your dark brown yarn in strands and use a single strand to embroider eyelashes over round 10.
- Split your coral yarn in strands and use a single strand to embroider a smile over round 11.
- Embroider rosy cheeks between rounds 10-11 using peach yarn, covering the width of 1 stitch.
- Tie the flower headband around the stamen frills on top of the head.

BODY AND STEM

→ *start in light peach yarn*

Pull up a loop of light peach yarn in the first leftover front loop of round 16 of the head (15). Start the first stitch in the same stitch where you attached the yarn.
Rnd 17: ch 1, FLO (sc in next st, inc in next st) repeat 6 times [18]
Change to coral yarn.
Rnd 18 – 20: sc in all 18 st [18]
Don't fasten off, but cut the coral yarn, leaving a 20"/ 50 cm long yarn tail.
Hold the upper skirt so the petals' wrong sides face inward. Insert the body, aligning the last round of the body with the last round of the upper skirt. Make sure that the first stitch is located in the middle of a petal (16).
Rnd 21: working through both layers of body and skirt, using the coral yarn tail, sc in all 18 st [18] (17)
Change to green yarn.
Rnd 22: BLO (sc in next 4 st, dec) repeat 3 times [15]
Stuff the body with fiberfill and continue stuffing the stem as you go.
Rnd 23: (sc in next 3 st, dec) repeat 3 times [12]
Rnd 24: (sc in next 2 st, dec) repeat 3 times [9]
Rnd 25 – 34: sc in all 9 st [9]
Rnd 35: (sc in next st, dec) repeat 3 times [6]
Fasten off, leaving a yarn tail.
Optional: *To make the stem sturdier and bendable, you can insert wire into it. Take a piece of wire and bend one end into an eyelet. Cut the wire to the length of the stem + 1 cm. Wrap the bent end with yarn, then carefully insert the wire into the stem.*
Using your yarn needle, weave the yarn tail through the front loop of each remaining stitch and pull it tight to close. Weave in the yarn end.

LOWER SKIRT AND SEPAL

→ *in green yarn*

Hold the flower upside down. Pull up a loop of green yarn in the first front loop left on round 21 (18). Start the first stitch in the same stitch where you attached the yarn.
Rnd 1: ch 1, FLO (sc in next 2 st, inc in next st) repeat 6 times [24]
Rnd 2: (sc in next 3 st, inc in next st) repeat 6 times [30]

In the next round, we will join the middle petals. Hold a middle petal with its right side facing you, start in the first stitch after the last stitch of round 4 19.

Note: *The middle petals should not align with the inner petals, but should be staggered, so that each one sits centered between two inner petals. If necessary, add a few sc to position the petal correctly.*

Rnd 3: work through both the lower skirt and the middle petal at once: (sc in next 6 st) repeat for 5 petals [30] 20 21

Take a moment to weave in the yarn tails of each petal. Thread a yarn tail onto your needle and sew together the bottom 3 stitches of 2 adjacent petals, then weave in the yarn end 22.

Continue crocheting the lower skirt.

Rnd 4: (sc in next 4 st, inc in next st) repeat 6 times [36]

Sc in next 4 st.

Note: *These additional sc stitches will ensure that the outer petals, which we will join in the next round, don't align with the middle petals.*

In the next round, we will join the outer petals. Hold an outer petal with its right side facing you, start in the stitch after the marked invisible join on round 4 23.

22

23

24

25

Rnd 5: (sc in next 6 st through both the lower skirt and the outer petal at once, sc in next st of the lower skirt only) repeat for 5 petals, sc in next st of the lower skirt [36] (24)
Continue making the sepals.
Rnd 6: (slst in next st, hdc in next st, dc inc in next st, tr inc in next st, dtr in next 4 st, tr inc in next st, dc inc in next st, hdc in next st, slst in next st) repeat 3 times [48]
Fasten off, and weave in the yarn end (25).

BIG LEAF
→ *in green yarn*

Ch 14. Stitches are worked around both sides of the foundation chain.

Rnd 1: start in second ch from hook, sc in next 3 ch, hdc in next ch, dc in next ch, tr in next 5 ch, dc in next ch, hdc in next ch, inc + ch-2-picot + inc in next ch.
Continue on the other side of the foundation chain, hdc in next ch, dc in next ch, tr in next 5 ch, dc in next ch, hdc in next ch, sc in next 3 ch [28]
Fasten off, leaving a long tail for sewing (26).

SMALL LEAF
→ *in green yarn*

Ch 11. Stitches are worked around both sides of the foundation chain.

26 27

28

29

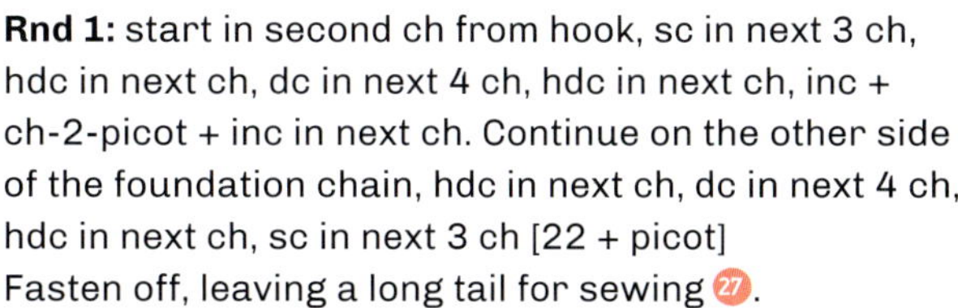

Rnd 1: start in second ch from hook, sc in next 3 ch, hdc in next ch, dc in next 4 ch, hdc in next ch, inc + ch-2-picot + inc in next ch. Continue on the other side of the foundation chain, hdc in next ch, dc in next 4 ch, hdc in next ch, sc in next 3 ch [22 + picot]
Fasten off, leaving a long tail for sewing (27).

ARM

→ *make 2, in light peach yarn*

Rnd 1: start 5 sc in a magic ring [5]
Rnd 2 – 10: sc in all 5 st [5]
Fasten off, leaving a long tail for sewing. The arms don't need to be stuffed.

WING

→ *make 2, in lime green yarn*

Ch 8. Crochet in rows.
Row 1: start in second ch from hook, slst in this ch, sc in next 3 ch, hdc in next 2 ch, hdc inc in next ch, ch 1, turn [8]
Row 2: sc in next st, inc in next st, sc in next 4 st, slst in next st, ch 1, turn [8] Leave the remaining stitch unworked.
Row 3: skip 1 st, slst in next st, sc in next st, inc in next st, 3 hdc in next st, ch 2, turn [7] Leave the remaining stitch unworked.
Row 4: hdc inc in next st, hdc in next 2 st, sc in next 2 st, slst in next st, ch 1, turn [7] Leave the remaining stitch unworked.
Row 5: skip 1 st, slst in next st, sc in next 2 st, inc in next st, hdc in next st, 3 dc in next st, ch 2, turn [9]
Row 6: slst in second ch from hook, sc in next 8 st [9]
Sc in next 4 row-ends until you reach the first ch of row 1, which was left unworked.
Fasten off, leaving a long tail for sewing (28).

ASSEMBLY

- Sew the leaves to the bottom of the lower skirt, positioning them in a gap between two sepals. The right side of the leaves should face downward (29).
- Flatten the arms and sew them to the body between rounds 17-18.
- Sew the wings to the back of the body, between rounds 18-19, 2 stitches apart.

REVERSIBLE **WITCH & CAULDRON**

SKILL LEVEL

★☆☆

SIZE

5.5" / 13.5 cm tall (witch side, with hat) or 2.75" / 7 cm tall (cauldron side) when made with the indicated yarn.

MATERIALS

- Sport weight yarn in:
    - pale green
    - purple
    - charcoal black
    - white
    - pink
    - black (leftover)
    - light pink (leftover)
- B-1 / 2.0 mm crochet hook
- Safety eyes (6 mm)
- Yarn needle
- Embroidery needle
- Stitch markers
- Scissors
- Fiberfill for stuffing

Scan or visit www.amigurumi.com/5303 to share pictures and find inspiration.

HEAD

→ *in pale green yarn*

Rnd 1: start 6 sc in a magic ring [6]
Rnd 2: inc in all 6 st [12]
Rnd 3: (sc in next st, inc in next st) repeat 6 times [18]
Rnd 4: (sc in next st, inc in next st, sc in next st) repeat 6 times [24]
Rnd 5: (sc in next 3 st, inc in next st) repeat 6 times [30]
Rnd 6: (sc in next 2 st, inc in next st, sc in next 2 st) repeat 6 times [36]
Rnd 7 – 14: sc in all 36 st [36]
Insert the safety eyes between rounds 11-12. The distance between the eyes should be 7 stitches ❶. Make sure that the beginning of the round is situated at the center back.
Rnd 15: (sc in next 4 st, dec) repeat 6 times [30]
Rnd 16: (sc in next 3 st, dec) repeat 6 times [24]
Rnd 17: (sc in next 2 st, dec) repeat 6 times [18]
Rnd 18: BLO (sc in next st, dec) repeat 6 times [12]
Stuff the head firmly with fiberfill.
Rnd 19: dec 6 times [6]
Fasten off, leaving a yarn tail. Using your yarn needle, weave the yarn tail through the front loop of each remaining stitch and pull it tight to close. Weave in the yarn end ❷.

BODY

→ *start in pale green yarn*

Pull up a loop of pale green yarn in the second front loop left on round 17 ❸. Work the first stitch in the same stitch where you attached the yarn.
Rnd 18: ch 1, FLO (sc in next 2 st, inc in next st) repeat 6 times [24]
Change to purple yarn.
Rnd 19 – 22: sc in all 24 st [24]
Fasten off with an invisible join. Weave in the yarn ends ❹.

CAULDRON/SKIRT

→ *in charcoal black yarn*

Rnd 1: start 6 sc in a magic ring [6]
Rnd 2: inc in all 6 st [12]
Rnd 3: (sc in next st, inc in next st) repeat 6 times [18]
Rnd 4: (sc in next st, inc in next st, sc in next st) repeat 6 times [24]

Stuff the body lightly with fiberfill.
In the next round we'll join the body to the skirt. Position the body on top of the skirt piece with the skirt's wrong side facing the body. Work the next round through both layers of skirt and body, using only the back loops on Rnd 22 of the body 5. The remaining front loops will be used to sew the petals to the skirt later. Finish stuffing before closing the seam.
Rnd 5: (sc in next 3 st, inc in next st) repeat 6 times [30]
Rnd 6: (sc in next 2 st, inc in next st, sc in next 2 st) repeat 6 times [36]
Rnd 7: (sc in next 5 st, inc in next st) repeat 6 times [42]
Rnd 8: (sc in next 3 st, inc in next st, sc in next 3 st) repeat 6 times [48]
Rnd 9: (sc in next 7 st, inc in next st) repeat 6 times [54]
Rnd 10: (sc in next 4 st, inc in next st, sc in next 4 st) repeat 6 times [60]
Rnd 11: (sc in next 19 st, inc in next st) repeat 3 times [63]
Rnd 12 – 20: sc in all 63 st [63]
Rnd 21 – 23: BLO sc in all 63 st [63]
Rnd 24: FLO (hdc in next 8 st, hdc inc in next st) repeat 7 times [70]
Fasten off with an invisible join. Weave in the yarn end 6.

CAULDRON HANDLE

→ make 2, in charcoal black yarn

Ch 15. Crochet in rows.
Row 1: start in second ch from hook, sc in all 14 ch [14]
Fasten off, leaving a long tail for sewing.

CAULDRON LEG

→ make 3, in charcoal black yarn

Rnd 1: start 6 sc in magic ring [6]
Rnd 2: sc in all 6 st [6]
Fasten off with an invisible join, leaving a long tail for sewing.

PETAL

→ *make 5, in purple yarn*

Ch 7. Stitches are worked around both sides of the foundation chain before switching to rows.
Row 1: start in second ch from hook, sc in next 5 ch, 3 sc in next ch. Continue on the other side of the foundation chain, sc in next 5 ch, ch 1, turn [13]
Row 2: sc in next 2 st, hdc in next 2 st, sc in next st, inc in next st, hdc in next st *(mark the stitch in which you worked the hdc with a stitch marker)*, ch 3, start in second ch from hook, slst in this ch, sc in next ch, hdc in the marked stitch where you worked the last hdc, inc in next st, sc in next st, hdc in next 2 st, sc in next 2 st [18]
Fasten off, leaving a long tail for sewing 7.

ARM

→ *make 2, start in pale green yarn*

Rnd 1: start 6 sc in a magic ring [6]
Rnd 2 – 6: sc in all 6 st [6]
Change to purple yarn.
Rnd 7 – 11: sc in all 6 st [6]
Fasten off, leaving a long tail for sewing. The arms don't need to be stuffed.

HAIR

→ *in pink yarn*

First, we make the hair base.
Rnd 1: start 7 sc in a magic ring [7]
Rnd 2: BLO hdc inc in next 7 st [14]
Rnd 3: BLO (hdc in next st, hdc inc in next st) repeat 7 times [21]
Rnd 4: BLO (hdc in next 2 st, hdc inc in next st) repeat 7 times [28]
Rnd 5: BLO (hdc in next 3 st, hdc inc in next st) repeat 7 times [35]
Rnd 6: BLO (hdc in next 6 st, hdc inc in next st) repeat 5 times [40]
Rnd 7 – 8: BLO hdc in all 40 st [40] 8
Continue to make the curls. Turn your work and crochet on the right side of your fabric, in the unworked front loops of the hair base 9.

Round of curls: (ch 10, start in second ch from hook, sc in next 9 ch, slst in next 3 front loops on the hair base) repeat until you reach the last front loop at the top of the hair base.
Fasten off and weave in the yarn end 10.

SKULL

→ *in white yarn*

Rnd 1: start 6 sc in a magic ring [6]
Rnd 2: inc in all 6 st [12]
Rnd 3: (sc in next st, inc in next st) repeat 6 times [18]
Rnd 4 – 5: sc in all 18 st [18]
Rnd 6: (sc in next st, dec) repeat 2 times, sc in next st, continue working in BLO, dec, sc in next st, dec, continue working in both loops, (sc in next st, dec) repeat 2 times [12]
Rnd 7: sc in all 12 st [12]
Fasten off with an invisible join, leaving a long tail for sewing.
Hold the skull with the last round facing you. Pull up a loop of white yarn in the rightmost leftover front loop

on round 5 (11).

Row of teeth: ch 1, skip 1 st, sc in next 3 st, ch 1, slst in last st [4]

Fasten off and weave in the yarn ends (12).

- With black yarn, embroider the eye cavities on round 4. The distance between the eye cavities should be 2 stitches.
- With black yarn, embroider a nose cavity on round 5.
- Split your black yarn in strands and use a single strand to embroider some vertical lines on the teeth row (13).

HAT

→ *start in charcoal black yarn*

Rnd 1: start 6 sc in a magic ring [6]

Rnd 2: sc in all 6 st [6]

Rnd 3: hdc inc in next 2 st, sc in next 4 st [8]

Rnd 4: sc in next st, hdc inc in next 2 st, hdc in next 5 st [10]

Rnd 5: sc in next 2 st, hdc inc in next 2 st, sc in next 4 st, inc in next st, sc in next st [13]

Rnd 6: sc in next 2 st, hdc in next 2 st, hdc inc in next st, hdc in next 2 st, sc in next 3 st, inc in next 2 st, sc in next st [16]

Rnd 7: sc in next 2 st, hdc in next 3 st, hdc inc in next st, hdc in next 3 st, sc in next 3 st, inc in next 2 st, sc in next 2 st [19]

Rnd 8: sc in next 5 st, inc in next st, sc in next 8 st, inc in next 3 st, sc in next 2 st [23]

Rnd 9: (sc in next 3 st, inc in next st) repeat 5 times, sc in next 2 st, inc in next st [29]

Rnd 10: sc in next 3 st, (inc in next st, sc in next st) repeat 4 times, sc in next 18 st [33]

Rnd 11: sc in next 3 st, (inc in next st, sc in next 3 st) repeat 3 times, sc in next 6 st, hdc in next 8 st, sc in next 4 st [36]

Rnd 12: sc in all 36 st [36]

Change to purple yarn, but don't fasten off the charcoal black yarn.

Rnd 13: BLO slst in all 36 st, slst in first st [36]

Continue working in joined rounds.

Rnd 14: ch 1, BLO sc in all 36 st, slst in first st [36]

Change to charcoal black yarn.

***Tip:** Work the slst in the next round rather loosely, so it's not too hard to work into them in Rnd 16.*

Rnd 15: BLO slst in all 36 st, slst in first st [36]

Rnd 16: ch 1, BLO (sc in next 5 st, inc in next st) repeat 6 times, slst in first st [42]

Rnd 17: ch 1, (sc in next 3 st, inc in next st, sc in next 3 st) repeat 6 times, slst in first st [48]

Rnd 18: ch 1, (sc in next 7 st, inc in next st) repeat 6 times, slst in first st [54]

Fasten off with an invisible join. Weave in the yarn end (14).

ASSEMBLY

- Shape the cauldron handle into a circle by sewing both ends together (15). Pin and sew a handle on each side of the cauldron, between rounds 22-23. Use the face of the witch as a guide when sewing them on (16).
- Pin and sew the cauldron legs to the bottom of the cauldron, between rounds 6-7, in a triangular formation. Position two legs at the front and the third leg at the back (17).
- Fold the cauldron down so that the wrong side is facing outward and the witch is revealed. Sew the flat side of the petals to the front loops left on round 22 of the body (18). 2 petals are at the front, the other 2 are on the sides, and the last petal is at the center back.
- Using black yarn, embroider 2 "X" shapes on the purple part of the body as lacing.
- Flatten the opening of the arms and sew them to the body, between rounds 19-20.
- Embroider rosy cheeks between rounds 12-13 of the head, using light pink yarn.
- Split your pink yarn in strands and use a single strand to embroider a smile on round 13.
- Using a new tail of pink yarn, sew the last round of the hair base to the head, the back side touching rounds 12-13 of the head, the front side between rounds 5-6.
- Stuff the skull lightly with fiberfill and sew it onto the curly hair (you can insert a strand of the curls inside the skull to make space to sew the skull on) (19) (20).
- Leave the hat removable.

REVERSIBLE **BABY DRAGON**

SKILL LEVEL

★★☆

SIZE

5.5" / 13.5 cm tall when made with the indicated yarn.

MATERIALS

- Sport weight yarn in:
  - turquoise
  - light beige
  - white
  - black
  - light purple
  - purple
  - teal
  - variegated/multicolored yarn for eggshell
- B-1 / 2.0 mm crochet hook
- Yarn needle
- Embroidery needle
- Stitch markers
- Scissors
- Fiberfill for stuffing

Scan or visit www.amigurumi.com/5304 to share pictures and find inspiration.

HEAD

→ *in turquoise yarn*

Rnd 1: start 6 sc in a magic ring [6]
Rnd 2: inc in all 6 st [12]
Rnd 3: (sc in next st, inc in next st) repeat 6 times [18]
Rnd 4: (sc in next st, inc in next st, sc in next st) repeat 6 times [24]
Rnd 5: (sc in next 3 st, inc in next st) repeat 6 times [30]
Rnd 6: (sc in next 2 st, inc in next st, sc in next 2 st) repeat 6 times [36]
Rnd 7: (sc in next 5 st, inc in next st) repeat 6 times [42]
Rnd 8: (sc in next 3 st, inc in next st, sc in next 3 st) repeat 6 times [48]
Rnd 9: (sc in next 7 st, inc in next st) repeat 6 times [54]
Rnd 10: (sc in next 4 st, inc in next st, sc in next 4 st) repeat 6 times [60]
Rnd 11: (sc in next 9 st, inc in next st) repeat 6 times [66]
Rnd 12 – 18: sc in all 66 st [66]
Rnd 19: (sc in next 5 st, inc in next st, sc in next 5 st) repeat 6 times [72]
Rnd 20: sc in all 72 st [72]
Rnd 21: sc in next 18 st, (sc in next st, inc in next st) repeat 3 times, sc in next 24 st, (inc in next st, sc in next st) repeat 3 times, sc in next 18 st [78]
Rnd 22 – 24: sc in all 78 st [78]
Rnd 25: (sc in next 11 st, dec) repeat 6 times [72]
Rnd 26: (sc in next 5 st, dec, sc in next 5 st) repeat 6 times [66]
Rnd 27: (sc in next 9 st, dec) repeat 6 times [60]
Rnd 28: (sc in next 4 st, dec, sc in next 4 st) repeat 6 times [54]
Rnd 29: (sc in next 7 st, dec) repeat 6 times [48]
Rnd 30: (sc in next 3 st, dec, sc in next 3 st) repeat 6 times [42]
Rnd 31: (sc in next 5 st, dec) repeat 6 times [36]
Rnd 32: (sc in next 2 st, dec, sc in next 2 st) repeat 6 times [30]
Stuff the head with fiberfill and continue stuffing as you go.
Rnd 33: BLO (sc in next 3 st, dec) repeat 6 times [24]
Rnd 34: (sc in next 2 st, dec) repeat 6 times [18]
Rnd 35: (sc in next st, dec) repeat 6 times [12]
Rnd 36: dec 6 times [6]
Fasten off, leaving a yarn tail. Using your yarn needle, weave the yarn tail through the front loop of each remaining stitch and pull it tight to close. Weave in the yarn end.

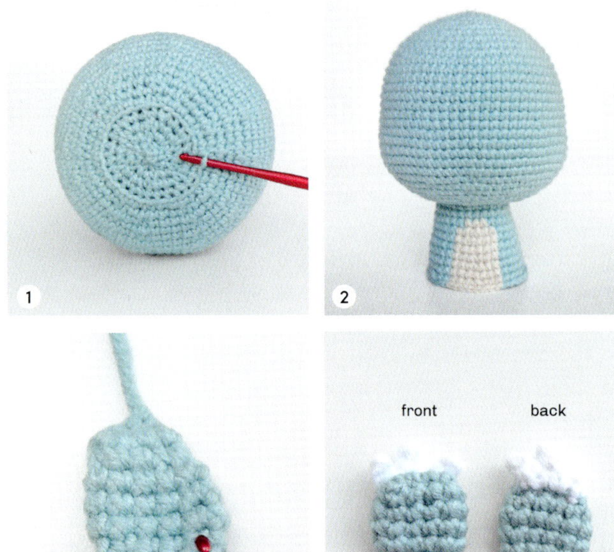

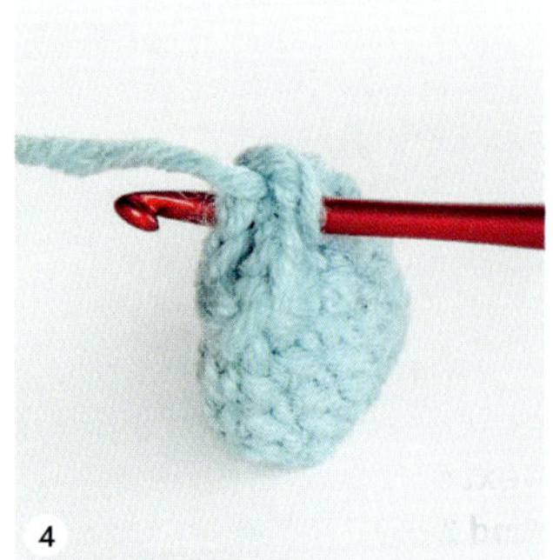

UPPER BODY

→ *start in turquoise yarn*

Hold the head upside down and pull up a loop of turquoise yarn in the last front loop left on round 32 ❶. Work the first stitch in the same stitch where you attached the yarn.
Rnd 33: ch 1, FLO sc in all 30 st [30]
Rnd 34: (sc in next 9 st, inc in next st) repeat 3 times [33]
Continue working with 2 colors, alternating turquoise and light beige yarn. The color change is indicated in italics.
Note: *I use the cut-and-tie technique (p. 17). It's a bit time-consuming, but limits tension issues or colors popping through.*
Rnd 35: *(turquoise)* sc in next 15 st, *(light beige)* sc in next 3 st, *(turquoise)* sc in next 15 st [33]
Rnd 36: *(turquoise)* sc in next 5 st, inc in next st, sc in next 8 st, *(light beige)* sc in next 2 st, inc in next st, sc in next 2 st, *(turquoise)* sc in next 8 st, inc in next st, sc in next 5 st [36]
Rnd 37: *(turquoise)* sc in next 15 st, *(light beige)* sc in next 6 st, *(turquoise)* sc in next 15 st [36]
Rnd 38: *(turquoise)* sc in next 11 st, inc in next st, sc in next 3 st, *(light beige)* sc in next 6 st, *(turquoise)* sc in next 2 st, inc in next st, sc in next 11 st, inc in next st [39]
Rnd 39: *(turquoise)* sc in next 16 st, *(light beige)* sc in next 6 st, *(turquoise)* sc in next 17 st [39]
Rnd 40: *(turquoise)* sc in next 6 st, inc in next st, sc in next 9 st, *(light beige)* sc in next 3 st, inc in next st, sc in next 2 st, *(turquoise)* sc in next 10 st, inc in next st, sc in next 6 st [42]
Rnd 41: *(turquoise)* sc in next 17 st, *(light beige)* sc in next 7 st, *(turquoise)* sc in next 18 st [42]
Rnd 42: *(turquoise)* (sc in next 6 st, inc in next st) repeat 2 times, sc in next 3 st, *(light beige)* sc in next 3 st, inc in next st, sc in next 3 st, cut the light beige yarn and leave a long tail for sewing, *(turquoise)* sc in next 3 st, inc in next st, (sc in next 6 st, inc in next st) repeat 2 times [48]
Fasten off with an invisible join, leaving a long tail for sewing ❷.

LOWER BODY

→ *start in turquoise yarn*

Leave a 4" / 10 cm long starting yarn tail, this will later be used to join the lower body and the eggshell together.
Rnd 1: start 6 sc in a magic ring [6]
Rnd 2: inc in all 6 st [12]
Rnd 3: (sc in next st, inc in next st) repeat 6 times [18]
Rnd 4: (sc in next st, inc in next st, sc in next st) repeat 6 times [24]
Rnd 5: (sc in next 3 st, inc in next st) repeat 6 times [30]
Rnd 6: (sc in next 2 st, inc in next st, sc in next 2 st) repeat 6 times [36]
Rnd 7: (sc in next 5 st, inc in next st) repeat 6 times [42]

Rnd 8: (sc in next 3 st, inc in next st, sc in next 3 st) repeat 6 times [48]
Continue working with 2 colors, alternating turquoise and light beige yarn. The color change is indicated in italics.
Rnd 9: *(turquoise)* (sc in next 7 st, inc in next st) repeat 2 times, sc in next 3 st, *(light beige)* sc in next 4 st, inc in next st, sc in next 3 st, *(turquoise)* sc in next 4 st, inc in next st, (sc in next 7 st, inc in next st) repeat 2 times [54]
Rnd 10: *(turquoise)* (sc in next 4 st, inc in next st, sc in next 4 st) repeat 2 times, sc in next 3 st, *(light beige)* sc in next st, inc in next st, sc in next 7 st, *(turquoise)* sc in next st, inc in next st, sc in next 4 st, (sc in next 4 st, inc in next st, sc in next 4 st) repeat 2 times [60]
Rnd 11: *(turquoise)* (sc in next 9 st, inc in next st) repeat 2 times, sc in next 3 st, *(light beige)* sc in next 6 st, inc in next st, sc in next 3 st, *(turquoise)* sc in next 6 st, inc in next st, (sc in next 9 st, inc in next st) repeat 2 times [66]
Rnd 12: *(turquoise)* (sc in next 5 st, inc in next st, sc in next 5 st) repeat 2 times, sc in next 3 st, *(light beige)* sc in next 2 st, inc in next st, sc in next 8 st, *(turquoise)* sc in next 2 st, inc in next st, sc in next 5 st, (sc in next 5 st, inc in next st, sc in next 5 st) repeat 2 times [72]
Rnd 13: *(turquoise)* (sc in next 11 st, inc in next st) repeat 2 times, sc in next 3 st, *(light beige)* sc in next 8 st, inc in next st, sc in next 3 st, *(turquoise)* sc in next 8 st, inc in next st, (sc in next 11 st, inc in next st) repeat 2 times [78]
Rnd 14 – 15: *(turquoise)* sc in next 29 st, *(light beige)* sc in next 13 st, *(turquoise)* sc in next 36 st [78]
Rnd 16 – 20: *(turquoise)* sc in next 29 st, *(light beige)* sc in next 14 st, *(turquoise)* sc in next 35 st [78]
Fasten off with an invisible join, leaving a long turquoise yarn tail for sewing ❸. This will later be used to sew the lower body and the eggshell together. Weave in the light beige yarn end.

FOOT

→ *make 2, in turquoise yarn*

Ch 5. Stitches are worked around both sides of the foundation chain.
Rnd 1: start in second ch from hook, sc in next 3 ch, 3 sc in next ch. Continue on the other side of the foundation chain, sc in next 2 ch, inc in next ch [10]
Rnd 2: sc in next 4 st, inc in next st, BLO sc in next 4 st, continue working in both loops, inc in next st [12]
Rnd 3 – 5: sc in all 12 st [12]
Rnd 6: dec, sc in next 2 st, dec 2 times, sc in next 2 st, dec [8]
The foot doesn't need to be stuffed. Flatten the foot and work the next round through both layers to close. Skip 1 stitch on either end of the foot opening.
Rnd 7: sc in next 3 st [3] ❹
Fasten off, leaving a long tail for sewing.

Hold the foot with the first round downward. Pull up a loop of white yarn in the rightmost front loop of round 1 ❺.
Row of nails: (ch 3, start in second ch from hook, slst in next 2 ch, slst in next front loop) repeat 3 times [3 nails]
Fasten off and weave in the yarn ends ❻.

LEFT FRONT LEG

→ *in turquoise yarn*

Ch 5. Stitches are worked around both sides of the foundation chain.
Rnd 1: start in second ch from hook, sc in next 3 ch, 3 sc in next ch. Continue on the other side of the foundation chain, sc in next 2 ch, inc in next ch [10]
Rnd 2: sc in next 4 st, inc in next st, BLO sc in next 4 st,

continue working in both loops, inc in next st [12]
Rnd 3: (sc in next 5 st, inc in next st) repeat 2 times [14]
Rnd 4: sc in all 14 st [14]
Rnd 5: sc in next 5 st, dec, sc in next 7 st [13]
Rnd 6 – 8: sc in next 5 st, dec, sc in next 5 st, inc in next st [13]
Rnd 9: sc in next 5 st, dec, sc in next 6 st [12]
Rnd 10: sc in next 10 st, dec [11]
Rnd 11: sc in next 5 st, dec, sc in next 4 st [10]
Rnd 12: sc in next 10 st [10]
Stuff the leg lightly with fiberfill — only about 30-40% of its length. Flatten the leg and work the next round through both layers to close. Skip 1 stitch on either end of the leg opening.
Rnd 13: sc in next 4 st [4] ❼
Fasten off, leaving a long tail for sewing.

RIGHT FRONT LEG

→ in turquoise yarn

Ch 5. Stitches are worked around both sides of the foundation chain.
Rnd 1: start in second ch from hook, sc in next 3 ch, 3 sc in next ch. Continue on the other side of the foundation chain, sc in next 2 ch, inc in next ch [10]
Rnd 2: BLO sc in next 4 st, continue working in both loops, inc in next st, sc in next 4 st, inc in next st [12]
Rnd 3: (sc in next 5 st, inc in next st) repeat 2 times [14]
Rnd 4: sc in all 14 st [14]
Rnd 5: sc in next 5 st, dec, sc in next 7 st [13]
Rnd 6 – 8: sc in next 5 st, dec, sc in next 5 st, inc in next st [13]
Rnd 9: sc in next 5 st, dec, sc in next 6 st [12]
Rnd 10: sc in next 10 st, dec [11]
Rnd 11: sc in next 5 st, dec, sc in next 4 st [10]
Rnd 12: sc in next 10 st [10]
Stuff the leg lightly with fiberfill — only about 30-40% of its length. Flatten the leg and work the next round through both layers to close. Skip 1 stitch on either end of the leg opening.
Rnd 13: sc in next 4 st [4]
Fasten off, leaving a long tail for sewing ❽.

Hold the front legs with the first round downward, both legs bending inward. Pull up a loop of white yarn in the rightmost front loop of round 1 ❾.
Row of nails: (ch 3, start in second ch from hook, slst in next 2 ch, slst in next front loop) repeat 3 times [3 nails]
Fasten off and weave in the yarn ends ❿.

SNOUT

→ in turquoise yarn

Ch 6. Stitches are worked around both sides of the foundation chain.
Rnd 1: start in second ch from hook, sc in next 4 ch, 3 sc in next ch. Continue on the other side of the foundation chain, sc in next 3 ch, inc in next ch [12]
Rnd 2: inc in next st, sc in next 3 st, inc in next 3 st, sc in next 3 st, inc in next 2 st [18]
Rnd 3: sc in next st, inc in next st, sc in next 3 st, (sc in next st, inc in next st) repeat 3 times, sc in next 3 st, (sc in next st, inc in next st) repeat 2 times [24]
Rnd 4: sc in all 24 st [24]
Rnd 5: sc in next 11 st [11] Leave the remaining

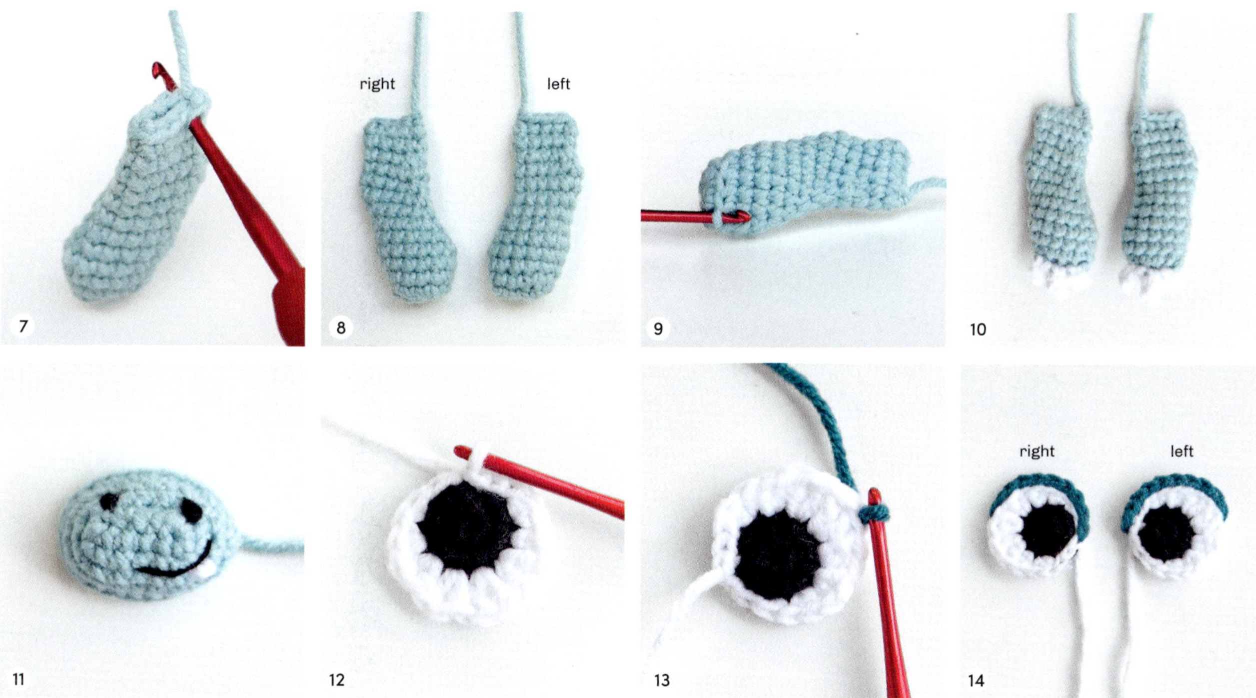

7 8 9 10 11 12 13 14

stitches unworked.
Fasten off with an invisible join, leaving a long tail for sewing.

Round 5 of the snout will be positioned downward when attached to the head. Keep this in mind for embroidery.

- Using black yarn, embroider the nostrils over round 2.
- Split your black yarn in strands and use a single strand to embroider a mouth.
- Embroider a fang using white yarn (11).

RIGHT EYE

→ *start in black yarn*

Rnd 1: start 6 sc in a magic ring [6]
Continue working in joined rounds.
Rnd 2: inc in all 6 st, slst in first st [12]
Change to white yarn.
Rnd 3: slst in next 2 st, sc in next st, inc in next st, hdc inc in next st, dc inc in next 3 st, hdc inc in next st, inc in next st, slst in next 2 st, slst in first st [19] (12)
Change to teal yarn. Cut the white yarn, leaving a long tail for sewing.
Rnd 4: BLO slst in next 10 st [10] Leave the remaining stitches unworked.
Fasten off and weave in the teal yarn end.

LEFT EYE

→ *start in black yarn*

Rnd 1: start 6 sc in a magic ring [6]
Continue working in joined rounds.
Rnd 2: inc in all 6 st, slst in first st [12]
Change to white yarn.
Rnd 3: slst in next 2 st, sc in next st, inc in next st, hdc inc in next st, dc inc in next 3 st, hdc inc in next st, inc in next st, slst in next 2 st, slst in first st [19]
Fasten off, leaving a long tail for sewing.
Starting from the last stitch, count 11 stitches backward and pull up a loop of teal yarn in the back loop of this stitch (13).
Rnd 4: BLO slst in next 10 st [10] Leave the remaining stitches unworked.
Fasten off and weave in the teal yarn end (14).

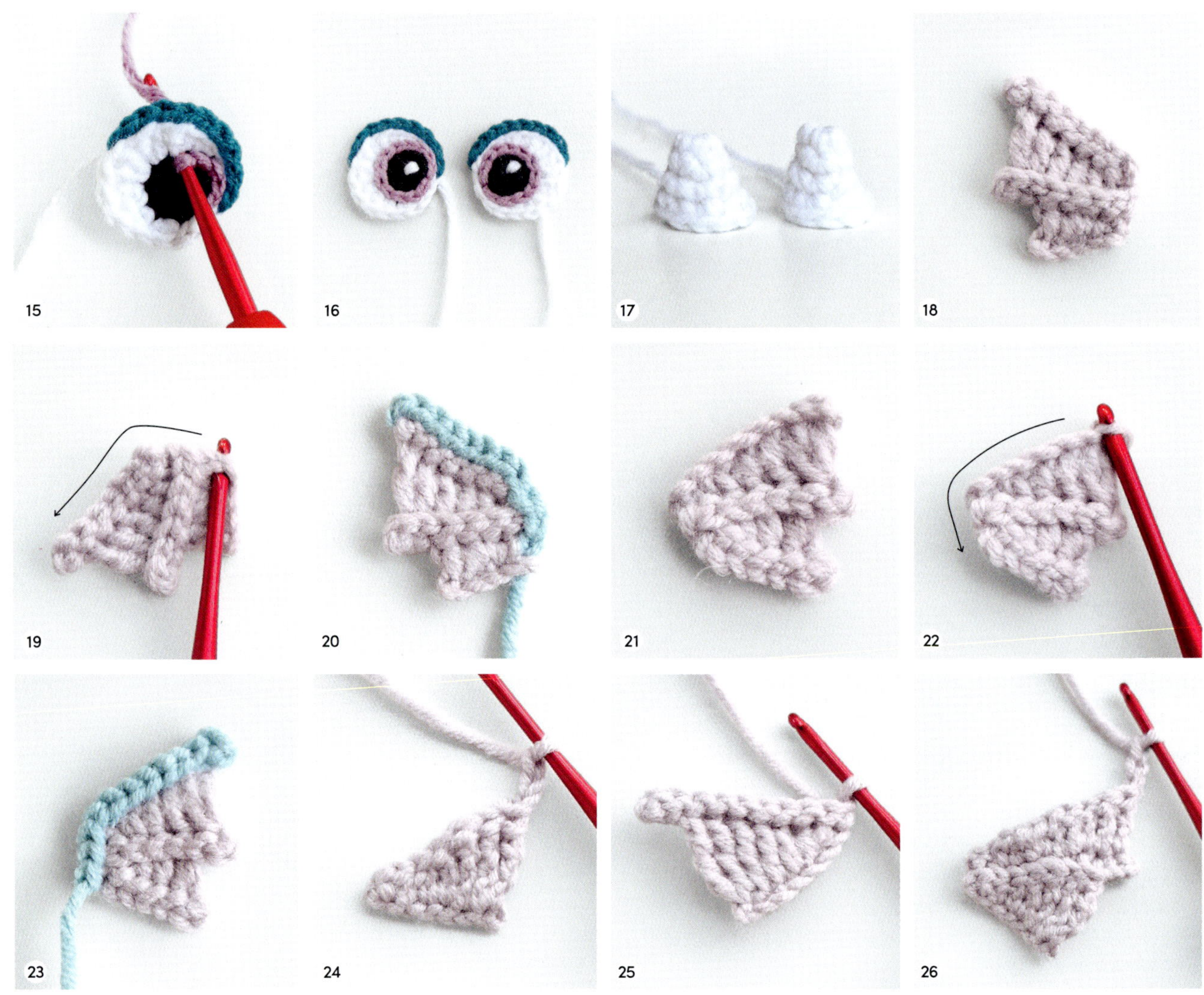

For both eyes: Using purple yarn, make 12 surface slip stitches between rounds 2 and 3 ⓯. Fasten off and weave in the yarn ends.
Using white yarn, embroider a flare on the eyes ⓰.

HORN

→ *make 2, in white yarn*

Rnd 1: start 4 sc in a magic ring [4]
Rnd 2: (sc in next st, inc in next st) repeat 2 times [6]
Rnd 3: (sc in next st, inc in next st) repeat 3 times [9]
Rnd 4: (sc in next 2 st, inc in next st) repeat 3 times [12]
Fasten off with an invisible join, leaving a long tail for sewing ⓱.

BIG SPIKE

→ *make 2, in teal yarn*

Rnd 1: start 6 sc in a magic ring [6]
Rnd 2: (sc in next 2 st, inc in next st) repeat 2 times [8]
Rnd 3: (sc in next 3 st, inc in next st) repeat 2 times [10]
Rnd 4: (sc in next 4 st, inc in next st) repeat 2 times [12]

Fasten off with an invisible join, leaving a long tail for sewing.

MEDIUM SPIKE

→ *make 2, in teal yarn*

Rnd 1: start 6 sc in a magic ring [6]
Rnd 2: (sc in next 2 st, inc in next st) repeat 2 times [8]
Rnd 3: (sc in next 3 st, inc in next st) repeat 2 times [10]
Fasten off with an invisible join, leaving a long tail for sewing.

SMALL SPIKE

→ *make 4, in teal yarn*

Rnd 1: start 6 sc in a magic ring [6]
Rnd 2: (sc in next 2 st, inc in next st) repeat 2 times [8]
Fasten off with an invisible join, leaving a long tail for sewing.

THIN SPIKE

→ *make 2, in teal yarn*

Ch 5. Crochet in rows.
Row 1: start in second ch from hook, sc in next ch, dc in next ch, tr in next ch, dtr in next ch [4]
Fasten off, leaving a long tail for sewing.

RIGHT EAR

→ *start in light purple yarn*

Ch 5. Crochet in rows.
Row 1: start in second ch from hook, slst in this ch, sc in next ch, hdc in next 2 ch, ch 3, turn [4]
Row 2: start in second ch from hook, slst in next 2 ch, BLO slst in next 4 st, ch 1, turn [6]
Row 3: work this row in BLO, slst in next st, sc in next st, hdc in next st, dc in next st, dc inc in next st, ch 2, turn [6] Leave the remaining stitch unworked.
Row 4: start in second ch from hook, slst in this ch, BLO slst in next 6 st [7]
Fasten off and weave in the yarn ends (18).
Pull up a loop of turquoise yarn in the first stitch of row 1 (19) and leave a long starting yarn tail for sewing.
Decorative round: slst in next 3 row-ends, slst in next 7 st of row 4.
Fasten off and weave in the yarn end (20).

LEFT EAR

→ *start in light purple yarn*

Ch 7. Crochet in rows.
Row 1: start in second ch from hook, slst in this ch, sc in next ch, hdc in next ch, dc in next ch, dc2tog, ch 2, turn [5]
Row 2: start in second ch from hook, slst in this ch, BLO slst in next 5 st, ch 1, turn [6]
Row 3: work this row in BLO, slst in next st, sc in next st, hdc in next 2 st, ch 2, turn [4] Leave the remaining stitches unworked.
Row 4: start in second ch from hook, slst in this ch, BLO slst in next 4 st [5]
Fasten off and weave in the yarn ends (21).
Pull up a loop of turquoise yarn in the first ch of the foundation chain (22).
Decorative round: ch 2, start in second ch from hook, slst in this ch, slst in the same stitch where you joined the yarn, slst in next 6 ch of the foundation chain, slst in next 3 row-ends.
Fasten off, leaving a long tail for sewing (23).

WING BONE

→ *make 2, in turquoise yarn*

Rnd 1: start 6 sc in a magic ring [6]
Rnd 2 – 10: sc in all 6 st [6]
Fasten off with an invisible join, leaving a long tail for sewing. The wing bone doesn't need to be stuffed.

RIGHT WING

→ *start in light purple yarn*

Ch 7. Crochet in rows.
Row 1: start in second ch from hook, sc in this ch, hdc in next ch, dc in next ch, tr in next ch, dtr in next ch, dtr inc in next ch, ch 3, turn [7] (24)
Row 2: start in second ch from hook, slst in next 2 ch, BLO slst in next 7 st, ch 1, turn [9] (25)
Row 3: work this row in BLO, slst in next st, sc in next st, hdc in next st, hdc inc in next st, dc in next st, dc inc in next st, tr in next 2 st, ch 3, turn [10] (26) Leave the

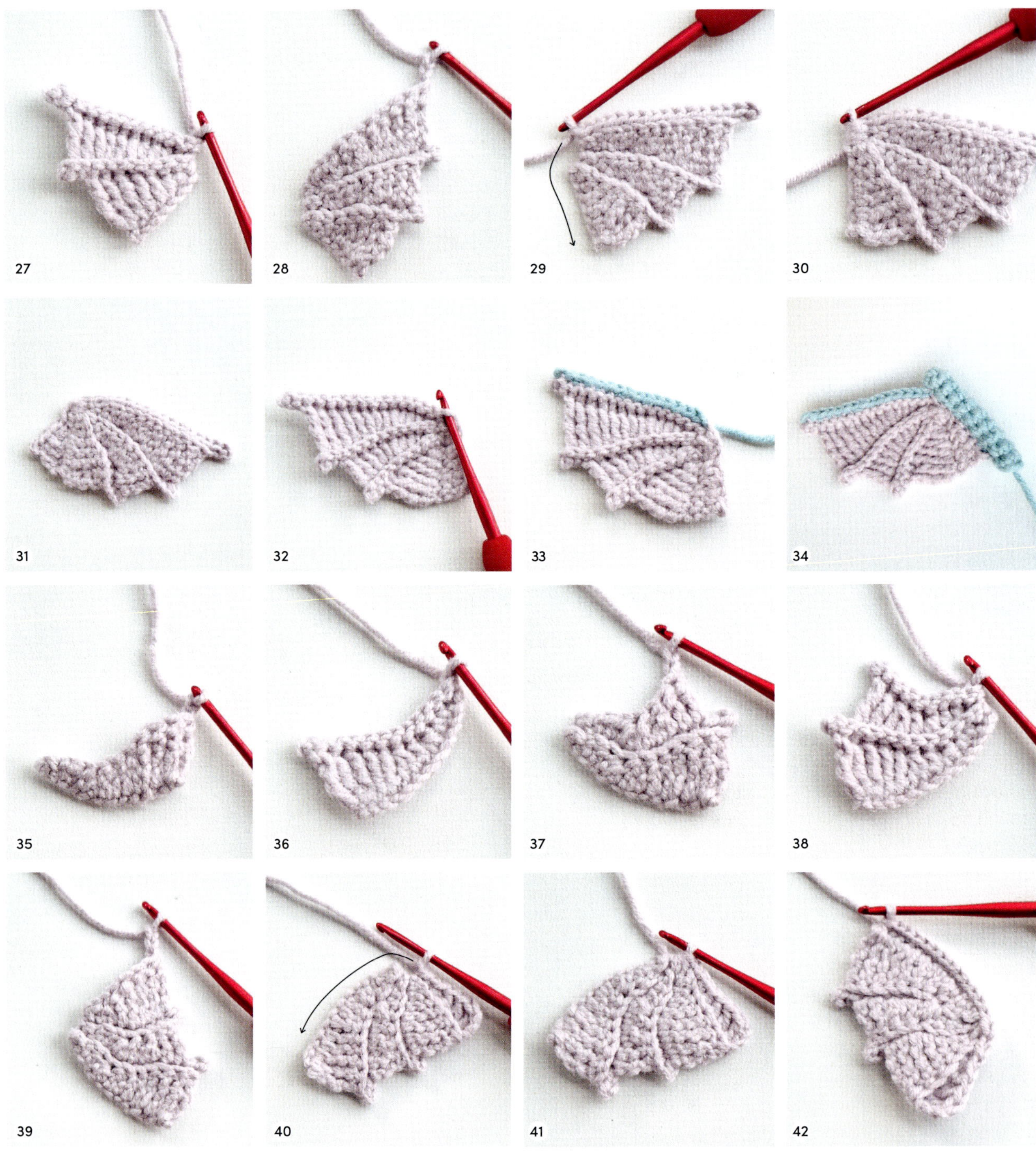

27
28
29
30
31
32
33
34
35
36
37
38
39
40
41
42

remaining stitch unworked.
Row 4: start in second ch from hook, slst in next 2 ch, BLO slst in all 10 st, ch 1, turn [12] 27
Row 5: work this row in BLO, slst in next st, sc in next st, hdc in next st, hdc inc in next st, dc in next st, dc inc in next st, tr in next 2 st, dtr in next 3 st, ch 3, turn [13] Leave the remaining stitch unworked 28.
Row 6: start in second ch from hook, slst in next 2 ch, BLO slst in all 13 st, ch 1 [15] 29
Decorative row: don't turn, hdc3tog in the row-ends 30, ch 1, continue crocheting in the foundation chain, slst in next ch, sc in next ch, hdc in next ch, dc in next 2 ch, tr in next ch [7] 31
Fasten off and weave in the yarn ends.

Hold the wing with its right side facing you. Leave a long starting yarn tail and pull up a loop of turquoise yarn in the rightmost stitch on the longest side of the wing (the last ch made in row 6) 32. Crochet along the upper side of the wing.
Row of lining: FLO slst in all 15 st [15]
Fasten off and weave in the yarn ends 33. Sew the wing bone to the wing, using the turquoise starting yarn tail 34.

LEFT WING

→ *start in light purple yarn*

Ch 14. Crochet in rows.
Row 1: start in second ch from hook, slst in this ch, sc in next ch, hdc in next ch, hdc2tog, dc in next ch, dc2tog, tr in next 2 ch, dtr in next 3 ch, ch 2, turn [11] 35
Row 2: start in second ch from hook, slst in this ch, BLO slst in next 11 st, ch 1, turn [12] 36
Row 3: work this row in BLO, slst in next st, sc in next st, hdc in next st, hdc2tog, dc in next st, dc2tog, tr in next 2 st, ch 2, turn [8] Leave the remaining stitches unworked 37.
Row 4: start in second ch from hook, slst in this ch, BLO slst in next 8 st, ch 1, turn [9] 38
Row 5: work this row in BLO, sc in next st, hdc in next st, dc in next st, tr in next st, dtr in next st, dtr2tog, ch 3, turn [6] Leave the remaining stitches unworked 39.
Row 6: work this row in BLO, tr in next st, dc in next 2 st, hdc in next st, sc in next st, slst in next st, ch 1 [6] 40
Decorative row: don't turn, hdc3tog in the row ends 41 *(mark this hdc3tog with a stitch marker)*, continue crocheting in the foundation chain, slst in next 13 ch [14] 42
Change to turquoise yarn.
Row of lining: ch 2, turn, start in second ch from hook, slst in this ch, BLO slst in next 14 st (until you reach the marked hdc3tog stitch) [15]
Fasten off, leaving a long tail for sewing 43.
Sew the wing bone to the wing, using the turquoise yarn tail 44.

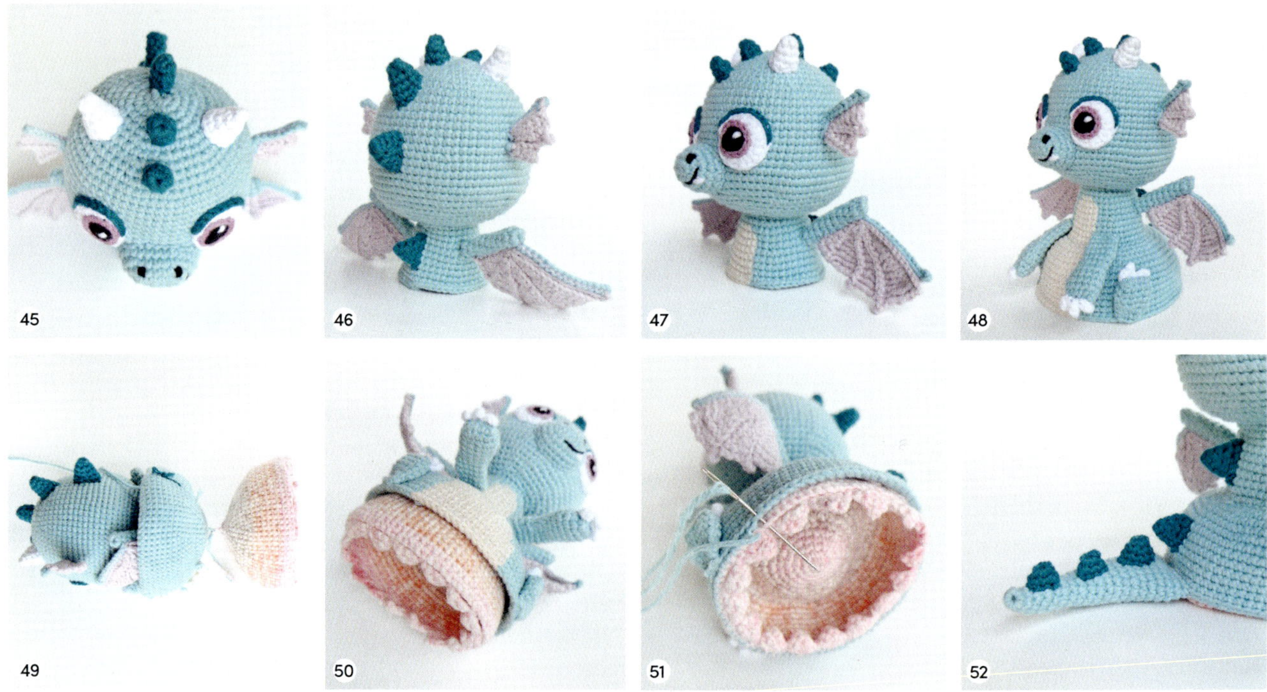

45 46 47 48 49 50 51 52

TAIL

→ *in turquoise yarn*

Rnd 1: start 6 sc in a magic ring [6]
Rnd 2: sc in all 6 st [6]
Rnd 3: inc in next st, sc in next st, hdc in next 2 st, sc in next st, inc in next st [8]
Rnd 4: sc in all 3 st, hdc in next 2 st, sc in next 2 st, inc in next st [9]
Rnd 5: sc in next 3 st, hdc in next 3 st, sc in next 3 st [9]
Rnd 6: sc in next 3 st, hdc in next 3 st, sc in next 2 st, inc in next st [10]
Rnd 7: inc in next st, sc in next 2 st, hdc in next 3 st, sc in next 4 st [11]
Rnd 8: sc in next 4 st, hdc in next 3 st, sc in next 3 st, inc in next st [12]
Rnd 9: inc in next st, sc in next 3 st, hdc in next 4 st, sc in next 4 st [13]
Rnd 10: sc in next 5 st, hdc in next 4 st, sc in next 3 st, inc in next st [14]
Rnd 11: inc in next st, sc in next 3 st, hdc in next 5 st, sc in next 5 st [15]
Rnd 12: sc in next 5 st, hdc in next 5 st, sc in next 4 st, inc in next st [16]
Rnd 13: inc in next st, sc in next 4 st, hdc in next 6 st, sc in next 5 st [17]
Rnd 14: sc in next 6 st, hdc in next 6 st, sc in next 4 st, inc in next st [18]
Rnd 15: inc in next st, sc in next 4 st, hdc in next 7 st, sc in next 6 st [19]
Rnd 16: sc in next 6 st, hdc in next 7 st, sc in next 5 st, inc in next st [20]
Rnd 17: inc in next st, sc in next 5 st, hdc in next 8 st, sc in next 6 st [21]
Rnd 18: sc in next 7 st, hdc in next 8 st, sc in next 5 st, inc in next st [22]
Rnd 19: sc in next 7 st, hdc in next 8 st, sc in next 7 st [22]
Rnd 20: sc in next 7 st, hdc in next 10 st, sc in next 2 st [19] Leave the remaining stitch unworked. Fasten off with an invisible join, leaving a long tail for sewing. Stuff the tail with fiberfill — for about 70% of its length.

EGGSHELL

→ in multicolored yarn

Leave a 4" / 10 cm long starting yarn tail, this will later be used to join the lower body and the eggshell together.
Rnd 1: start 6 sc in a magic ring [6]
Rnd 2: inc in all 6 st [12]
Rnd 3: (sc in next st, inc in next st) repeat 6 times [18]
Rnd 4: (sc in next st, inc in next st, sc in next st) repeat 6 times [24]
Rnd 5: (sc in next 3 st, inc in next st) repeat 6 times [30]
Rnd 6: (sc in next 2 st, inc in next st, sc in next 2 st) repeat 6 times [36]
Rnd 7: (sc in next 5 st, inc in next st) repeat 6 times [42]
Rnd 8: (sc in next 3 st, inc in next st, sc in next 3 st) repeat 6 times [48]
Rnd 9: (sc in next 7 st, inc in next st) repeat 6 times [54]
Rnd 10: (sc in next 4 st, inc in next st, sc in next 4 st) repeat 6 times [60]
Rnd 11: (sc in next 9 st, inc in next st) repeat 6 times [66]
Rnd 12: (sc in next 5 st, inc in next st, sc in next 5 st) repeat 6 times [72]
Rnd 13: (sc in next 11 st, inc in next st) repeat 6 times [78]
Rnd 14 – 20: sc in all 78 st [78]
Rnd 21: (ch 4, start in second ch from hook, sc in this ch, dc in next ch, tr in next ch, skip next 4 st, FLO slst in next st) repeat 15 times, ch 3, start in second ch from hook, slst in this ch, hdc in next ch, skip next 2 st, FLO slst in next st [16 ridges]
Fasten off and weave in the yarn end.

ASSEMBLY

- Sew the snout to the head between rounds 20-25. Stuff it with fiberfill before closing the seam.
- Sew the eyes to the head between rounds 15-21. The distance between the eyes should be 7 stitches. Position the eyes so the narrower white part is at the center of the face and the teal line is at the top.
- Stuff the horns lightly with fiberfill and sew them to the head, between rounds 6-8 (45).
- Sew the ears to the head between rounds 15-17. The distance between the ear and eye should be 7 stitches.
- Sew 2 small spikes to the head, between rounds 4-5 and between rounds 9-10. Sew a medium spike to the head, between rounds 1-4. Sew 2 big spikes to the head, between rounds 8-12 and between rounds 16-20 (45) (46).
- Sew a thin spike to the upper body, between rounds 37-41 (46).
- Sew the wing bones to the upper body (don't flatten, sew it 2 x 2 stitches wide), between rounds 36-37 (46) (47). The distance between the wings should be 10 stitches. The right side of the wings faces forward.
- Sew the front legs to the upper body, between rounds 40-41, right next to the belly. The nails face outward.
- Stuff the upper body with fiberfill and sew it to the lower body between rounds 8-9. Make sure the belly part of both upper and lower body match up. Sew the belly part first using the light beige yarn tail, then sew the rest using the turquoise yarn tail.
- Sew a thin spike to the lower body, between rounds 13-17.
- Sew the feet to the lower body, between rounds 18-20, the distance between foot and belly should be 5 stitches. The side with the nails is directed towards the body (48).

JOINING DRAGON'S BODY & EGGSHELL

Flip the dragon's lower body and the eggshell inside out, so that the wrong sides of both are outward. Make a knot with the yarn tails left from the magic rings. Try to leave a small space between both pieces (49).
Flip the dragon's body back, so the right side is outward. Don't flip the eggshell back, but keep it with the wrong side outward. The pieces don't need to be stuffed. Gently push the eggshell inside the body (50).
With the turquoise yarn tail left on the lower body, sew the last rounds of both pieces together, using only the back loops on both rounds for sewing (51).

ATTACHING DRAGON'S TAIL

Stuff the tail and flatten the last round. Sew the top 11 stitches of the tail to the front loops of round 20 of the lower body, and the remaining 11 stitches to the front loops of round 20 of the eggshell.
Sew the spikes to the tail, 2 small spikes between rounds 3-5 and rounds 9-11, and a medium spike between rounds 14-17 (52).

REVERSIBLE **SUNFLOWER FAIRY**

SKILL LEVEL

★★☆

SIZE

3.5" / 9 cm tall when made with the indicated yarn.

MATERIALS

- Sport weight yarn in:
    - dark brown
    - green
    - light peach
    - yellow
    - light brown
    - off-white
    - pink (leftover)
    - black (leftover)
    - red (leftover)
- B-1 / 2.0 mm crochet hook
- Yarn needle
- Embroidery needle
- Stitch marker
- Fiberfill for stuffing
- Scissors
- Optional: flower wire (gauge #22, 3"/7 cm long)
- Optional: pliers

Scan or visit www.amigurumi.com/5305 to share pictures and find inspiration.

UPPER PETAL

→ *make 10, in yellow yarn*

Ch 14. Stitches are worked around both sides of the foundation chain before switching to rows.

Row 1: start in second ch from hook, sc in next 9 ch, hdc in next 3 ch, 4 sc in next ch. Continue on the other side of the foundation ch, hdc in next 3 ch, sc in next 9 ch, ch 1, turn [28]

Row 2: sc in next 11 st, hdc in next 2 st, 3 hdc in each of next 2 st, hdc in next 2 st, sc in next 11 st [32]

Fasten off and weave in the yarn ends on 9 petals.

Don't fasten off on the tenth petal. Continue making the skirt.

SKIRT

→ *in yellow yarn*

Make the skirt by joining 10 petals. Crochet 5 sc in the row-ends on the flat side of each petal (1). The first 2 stitches and the last 2 stitches will be crocheted through 2 layers of 2 adjacent petals at once (2) (3).

Continue crocheting with the yellow yarn from the tenth petal. Hold the petal with the right side facing you. Hold another petal below the tenth petal, so that the first 2 stitches of the tenth petal are worked through both layers.

Rnd 1: ch 1, sc in next 2 st through both petals (4), sc in next st on tenth petal only. Hold another petal on top of the tenth petal and sc in next 2 st through both petals (5) (6), sc in next st on the new petal.

Repeat until all 10 petals are joined together (7).

To join the skirt in the round, position the last petal below the first petal, and sc in next 2 st through both layers (8), sc in next st on the first petal [30] (9)

***Note:** For the next 2 rounds, use regular decreases instead of invisible decreases. An invisible decrease is worked in the front loops only. As both sides of the final work will be visible, I prefer using a regular decrease (sc2tog), worked through both loops.*

Rnd 2: (sc in next 3 st, sc2tog) repeat 6 times [24]

Rnd 3: (sc in next 2 st, sc2tog) repeat 6 times [18]

Fasten off with an invisible join and weave in the yarn end (10).

5 4 3 2 1
1
2
3
4
5
6
7
8
9
10
11
12
13
14
15
16

HEAD

→ *start in dark brown yarn*

Rnd 1: start 6 sc in a magic ring [6]
Rnd 2: inc in all 6 st [12]
Rnd 3: (sc in next st, inc in next st) repeat 6 times [18]
Rnd 4: (sc in next st, inc in next st, sc in next st) repeat 6 times [24]
Rnd 5: (sc in next 3 st, inc in next st) repeat 6 times [30]
Rnd 6: (sc in next 2 st, inc in next st, sc in next 2 st) repeat 6 times [36]
Rnd 7: sc in all 36 st [36]
Continue working with 2 colors, alternating light peach and dark brown yarn. The color change is indicated in italics.
***Note:** I use the cut-and-tie technique (p. 17). It's a bit time-consuming, but limits tension issues or colors popping through.*
Rnd 8: work this round in BLO, *(dark brown)* sc in next 15 st, *(light peach)* sc in next 6 st, *(dark brown)* sc in next 15 st [36]
Rnd 9: *(dark brown)* BLO sc in next 13 st, continue working in both loops, sc in next st, *(light peach)* sc in next 9 st, *(dark brown)* sc in next st, BLO sc in next 12 st [36]
Rnd 10 – 12: *(dark brown)* sc in next 13 st, *(light peach)* sc in next 11 st, *(dark brown)* sc in next 12 st [36]
Rnd 13: *(dark brown)* (sc in next 4 st, dec) repeat 2 times, sc in next 2 st, *(light peach)* sc in next 2 st, dec, sc in next 4 st, dec, *(dark brown)* (sc in next 4 st, dec) repeat 2 times [30]
Rnd 14: *(dark brown)* (sc in next 3 st, dec) repeat 2 times, sc in next 2 st, *(light peach)* sc in next st, dec, sc in next 3 st, dec, *(dark brown)* (sc in next 3 st, dec) repeat 2 times [24]
Rnd 15: *(dark brown)* (sc in next 2 st, dec) repeat 2 times, sc in next 2 st, *(light peach)* dec, sc in next 2 st, dec, *(dark brown)* (sc in next 2 st, dec) repeat 2 times [18]
Continue in dark brown yarn.
Rnd 16: (sc in next st, dec) repeat 6 times [12]
Stuff the head firmly with fiberfill.
Rnd 17: BLO dec 6 times [6]
Fasten off, leaving a yarn tail. Using your yarn needle, weave the yarn tail through the front loop of each remaining stitch and pull it tight to close. Weave in the yarn end 11.

HEAD GARLAND 

→ *in light brown yarn*

Hold the head with its right side facing you. Pull up a loop of light brown yarn in the first front loop left on round 8 13. Work the first decorative round in the remaining front loops of rounds 8 and 7. Work the first slip stitch in the second front loop.
First decorative round: FLO (ch 4, slst in next st) repeat 48 times.
Fasten off and weave in the yarn ends.

Pull up a loop of light brown yarn in the last front loop left on round 8, at the back of the head.
Second decorative round: FLO (ch 4, slst in next st) repeat 11 times.
Fasten off and weave in the yarn ends 14.

EMBROIDERY FOR HAIR & FACE

- Embroider bangs between rounds 8-12 of the face, covering both the left and right sides, with a few strands extending over the forehead.
- Embroider eyes using black yarn, over round 11, about 5 stitches apart.
- Split your black yarn in strands and use a single strand to embroider eyelashes over round 11.

- Split your red yarn in strands and use a single strand to embroider a smile over round 12.
- Embroider rosy cheeks, with a width of 1 stitch, between rounds 11-12, using pink yarn.

BODY AND STEM

→ *start in light peach yarn*

Pull up a loop of light peach yarn in the first front loop left on round 16 of the head (15). Work the first stitch in the same stitch where you attached the yarn.
Rnd 17: FLO (sc in next st, inc in next st) repeat 6 times [18]
Change to yellow yarn.
Rnd 18 – 19: sc in all 18 st [18]
Don't fasten off, but cut the yellow yarn, leaving a 25"/ 60 cm long yarn tail.
Flip the skirt so the petals' wrong sides face inward. Insert the body, aligning the last round of the body with the last round of the skirt (16).
Rnd 20: working through both loops of the skirt and the front loops of the body, using the yellow yarn tail, sc in all 18 st [18] (17)
Change to green yarn.
Rnd 21: BLO sc in all 18 st [18]
Rnd 22: (sc in next 4 st, dec) repeat 3 times [15]
Stuff the body and stem with fiberfill and continue stuffing as you go.
Rnd 23: (sc in next 3 st, dec) repeat 3 times [12]
Rnd 24: (sc in next 2 st, dec) repeat 3 times [9]
Rnd 25 – 33: sc in all 9 st [9]
Rnd 34: (sc in next st, dec) repeat 3 times [6]
Fasten off, leaving a yarn tail.
Optional: *To make the stem sturdier and bendable, you can insert wire into it. Take a piece of wire and bend one end into an eyelet. Cut the wire to approx. the same length as the stem + body. Wrap the bent end with yarn, then carefully insert the wire into the stem* (18).
Using your yarn needle, weave the yarn tail through the front loop of each remaining stitch and pull it tight to close. Weave in the yarn end.

LOWER PETAL

→ *make 10, in yellow yarn*

Ch 7. Stitches are worked around both sides of the foundation chain before switching to rows.

Row 1: start in second ch from hook, sc in next 2 ch, hdc in next 3 ch, 4 sc in next ch. Continue on the other side of the foundation ch, hdc in next 3 ch, sc in next 2 ch, ch 1, turn [14]
Row 2: sc in next 3 st, hdc in next 3 st, 3 hdc in next 2 st, hdc in next 3 st, sc in next 3 st [18]
Fasten off and weave in the yarn ends.

INNER SKIRT & SEPALS

in green yarn

Hold the flower upside down. Pull up a loop of green yarn in the fourth front loop left on round 20 of the stem 19. Work the first stitch in the same stitch where you attached the yarn.
Rnd 1: ch 1, FLO (sc in next 2 st, inc in next st) repeat 6 times [24]
Rnd 2: (sc in next 7 st, inc in next st) repeat 3 times [27]
Rnd 3: (sc in next 4 st, inc in next st, sc in next 4 st) repeat 3 times [30]
Rnd 4: (sc in next 9 st, inc in next st) repeat 3 times [33]
Rnd 5: (sc in next 5 st, inc in next st, sc in next 5 st) repeat 3 times [36]
Rnd 6: (sc in next 11 st, inc in next st) repeat 3 times [39]
Rnd 7: (sc in next 6 st, inc in next st, sc in next 6 st) repeat 3 times [42]
Rnd 8: (sc in next 13 st, inc in next st) repeat 3 times [45]
Rnd 9: (sc in next 7 st, inc in next st, sc in next 7 st) repeat 3 times [48]
Rnd 10: (sc in next 23 st, inc in next st) repeat 2 times [50]
Rnd 11: FLO sc in all 50 st [50]
Next, we join the lower petals with the inner skirt by crocheting both layers together. Hold a lower petal with its flat side lined with the stitches of round 11 and its right side facing outward 20. Work 5 sc in the row-ends on the flat side of each petal 21.
Rnd 12: crochet through both layers of petal and skirt, (5 sc in each petal) repeat for all 10 petals [50] 22
Turn and flip the skirt so the wrong side is facing you. Continue making the sepals.
Sepals: ch 4, start in second ch from hook, slst in next 2 ch, sc in next ch, skip 2 st on the inner skirt, slst in next 2 st on the inner skirt, (ch 4, start in second ch from hook, slst in next 2 ch, sc in next ch, skip 1 st on

25 26

27

28

the inner skirt, slst in next 2 st on the inner skirt) repeat 32 times [33 sepals]

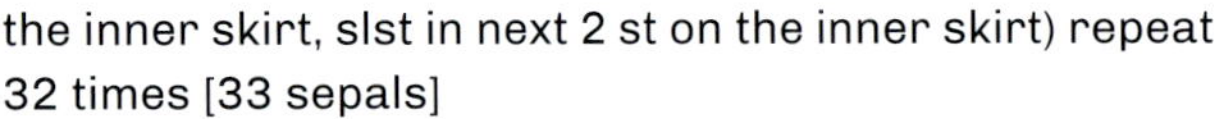

Fasten off and weave in the yarn ends 23 24.

LEAF

in green yarn

Rnd 1: start 7 sc in a magic ring [7]
Rnd 2: slst + ch 1 + hdc in next st, hdc inc in next st, 3 dc in next st, tr inc + ch-2-picot + tr inc in next st, 3 dc in next st, hdc inc in next 2 st, ch 1, slst in first st.
Fasten off, leaving a long tail for sewing 25.

ARM

make 2, start in light brown yarn

Rnd 1: start 5 sc in a magic ring [5]
Rnd 2 – 4: sc in all 5 st [5]
Change to light peach yarn.
Rnd 5 – 9: sc in all 5 st [5]
Fasten off, leaving a long tail for sewing.

WING

make 2, in off-white yarn

Ch 6. Stiches are worked around both sides of the foundation chain.
Rnd 1: start in second ch from hook, slst in this ch, sc in next ch, hdc in next ch, dc in next ch, 7 dc in next ch. Continue on the other side of the foundation chain, dc in next ch, hdc in next ch, sc in next ch, slst in next ch [15]
Fasten off, leaving a long tail for sewing. Pass the yarn tail to the first slst to make the tip more pointy 26.

ASSEMBLY

- Flatten the arms and sew them to the body, between rounds 17-18.
- Sew the wings over rounds 18-19, at the back of the body, with the wrong side facing the body 27.
- Sew the leaf to the stem 28.

REVERSIBLE **CINDERELLA**

SKILL LEVEL

★☆☆

SIZE

4.5" / 12 cm tall when made with the indicated yarn.

MATERIALS

- Sport weight yarn in:
  - light peach
  - off-white
  - baby blue
  - light brown
  - ecru
  - dark brown
  - light gray
  - peach (leftover)
  - pink (leftover)
  - blue (leftover)
- B-1 / 2.25 mm crochet hook
- Yarn needle
- Embroidery needle
- Stitch markers
- Fiberfill for stuffing
- 2 pairs of safety eyes (6mm)
- Scissors
- Optional: small plastic beads in blue and white
- Optional: multifunctional glue

Scan or visit www.amigurumi.com/5306 to share pictures and find inspiration.

***Note:** For this type of reversible amigurumi, it's recommended to crochet the stitches a bit more loosely. I use a 2.25 mm crochet hook here instead of a 2 mm crochet hook. By sizing up my crochet hook, I can achieve a more relaxed tension, making it easier to flip the characters at the end.*

CINDERELLA IN PRINCESS GOWN

HEAD

→ *in light peach yarn*

Rnd 1: start 6 sc in a magic ring [6]
Rnd 2: inc in all 6 st [12]
Rnd 3: (sc in next st, inc in next st) repeat 6 times [18]
Rnd 4: (sc in next st, inc in next st, sc in next st) repeat 6 times [24]
Rnd 5: (sc in next 3 st, inc in next st) repeat 6 times [30]
Rnd 6 – 8: sc in all 30 st [30]
Rnd 9: (sc in next 9 st, inc in next st) repeat 3 times [33]
Rnd 10 – 14: sc in all 33 st [33]
Insert the safety eyes between rounds 11-12. The distance between the eyes should be 7 stitches. Make sure that the beginning of the round is situated at the center back.
Rnd 15: (sc in next 9 st, dec) repeat 3 times [30]
Rnd 16: (sc in next 3 st, dec) repeat 6 times [24]
Rnd 17: (sc in next 2 st, dec) repeat 6 times [18]
Rnd 18: (sc in next st, dec) repeat 6 times [12]
Stuff the head firmly with fiberfill.
Rnd 19: BLO dec 6 times [6]
Fasten off, leaving a yarn tail. Using your yarn needle, weave the yarn tail through the front loop of each remaining stitch and pull it tight to close. Weave in the yarn end.

- Embroider rosy cheeks between rounds 12-13 using peach yarn.
- Split your pink yarn in strands and use a single strand to embroider a smile on round 13 ❶.

BODY

→ *start in light peach yarn*

Hold the head upside down and pull up a loop of light peach yarn in the second front loop left on round 18 ❷. Work the first stitch in the same stitch where you attached the yarn.
Rnd 19: ch 1, FLO (sc in next st, inc in next st) repeat 6 times [18]
Rnd 20: (sc in next 5 st, inc in next st) repeat 3 times [21]
Change to baby blue yarn.
Rnd 21 – 22: sc in all 21 st [21]

Rnd 23: (sc in next 6 st, inc in next st) repeat 3 times [24]
Fasten off with an invisible join, leaving a long tail for sewing 3.

ARM

→ *make 2, start in off-white yarn*

Rnd 1: start 5 sc in a magic ring [5]
Rnd 2 – 6: sc in all 5 st [5]
Change to light peach yarn.
Rnd 7 – 11: sc in all 5 st [5]
Fasten off, leaving a long tail for sewing. The arms don't need to be stuffed.

OFF-SHOULDER STRAP

→ *in off-white yarn*

Ch 27. Crochet in rows.
Row 1: start in second ch from hook, slst in all 26 ch [26]
Fasten off, leaving a long tail for sewing. Using your yarn needle, pass the tail through the last chain to make the tip tapered 4.

HAIR

→ *in light brown yarn*

Rnd 1: start 6 sc in a magic ring [6]
Rnd 2: inc in all 6 st [12]
Rnd 3: (sc in next st, inc in next st) repeat 6 times [18]
Rnd 4: (sc in next st, inc in next st, sc in next st) repeat 6 times [24]
Rnd 5: (sc in next 3 st, inc in next st) repeat 6 times [30]
Rnd 6: (sc in next 2 st, inc in next st, sc in next 2 st) repeat 6 times [36]
Rnd 7 – 10: sc in all 36 st [36]
Rnd 11: sc in next 14 st, slst in next st, continue making the hair strands,
Strand 1 – 2: (ch 10, start in second ch from hook, sc in all 9 ch, continue on the hair base, slst in next st) repeat 2 times,
Strand 3 – 5: (ch 9, start in second ch from hook, sc in all 8 ch, continue on the hair base, slst in next st) repeat 3 times,
Strand 6: ch 10, start in second ch from hook, sc in all 9 ch,

Continue on the hair base, slst in next st, sc in next 15 st [36 + 6 strands]
Fasten off with an invisible join, leaving a long tail for sewing.
Flip the hair base inside out, so that the wrong side is facing outward ❺. Hide the starting yarn tail on the inside by passing it through the magic ring.

HAIR BUN

→ *in light brown yarn*

Rnd 1: start 6 sc in a magic ring [6]
Rnd 2: inc in all 6 st [12]
Rnd 3: (sc in next st, inc in next st) repeat 6 times [18]
Rnd 4: (sc in next st, inc in next st, sc in next st) repeat 6 times [24]
Rnd 5: (sc in next 7 st, inc in next st) repeat 3 times [27]
Rnd 6: sc in all 27 st [27]
Rnd 7: (sc in next 7 st, dec) repeat 3 times [24]

Fasten off with an invisible join, leaving a long tail for sewing.
Flip the hair bun inside out, so that the wrong side is facing outward. Hide the starting yarn tail on the inside by passing it through the magic ring.

TIARA ❻

→ *in light gray yarn*

Ch 6. Crochet in rows.
Row 1: start in second ch from hook, slst in this ch, ch 2, slst in next ch on the foundation chain, sc + ch-2-picot + sc in next ch, slst in next ch, ch 2, slst in next ch on the foundation chain.
Fasten off, leaving a long tail for sewing ❼.
Optional: Decorate the wrong side of the tiara with beads.

SKIRT

→ *start in baby blue yarn*

Leave a 4" / 10 cm long starting yarn tail, this will later be used to join both Cinderellas together.
Rnd 1: start 6 sc in a magic ring [6]
Rnd 2: inc in all 6 st [12]
Rnd 3: (sc in next st, inc in next st) repeat 6 times [18]
Rnd 4: (sc in next st, inc in next st, sc in next st) repeat 6 times [24]
Rnd 5: (sc in next 3 st, inc in next st) repeat 6 times [30]
Rnd 6: (sc in next 2 st, inc in next st, sc in next 2 st) repeat 6 times [36]
Rnd 7: (sc in next 5 st, inc in next st) repeat 6 times [42]
Rnd 8: (sc in next 3 st, inc in next st, sc in next 3 st) repeat 6 times [48]
Rnd 9 – 10: sc in all 48 st [48]
Rnd 11: (sc in next 7 st, inc in next st) repeat 6 times [54]
Rnd 12 – 16: sc in all 54 st [54]
Rnd 17: (sc in next 4 st, inc in next st, sc in next 4 st) repeat 6 times [60]
Rnd 18 – 22: sc in all 60 st [60]
Change to off-white yarn. Don't fasten off the baby blue yarn, but bring the yarn tail to the outside.
Rnd 23: BLO (sc in next 9 st, inc in next st) repeat 6 times [66]
Rnd 24: sc in all 66 st [66]

9

10

11

12

Next, we make a round of frills. Since the wrong side of the frills should face outward, you turn your crochet-work, and work round 25 in BLO ❽.

Rnd 25: work this round in BLO, skip first st, sc in next st, hdc inc in next st, sc in next st, (slst in next st, sc in next st, hdc inc in next st, sc in next st) repeat 15 times, slst in next 2 st [81]

Slst in next st. Fasten off and weave in the yarn end.

Hold the skirt with the open side downward, facing you. Pull up a loop of the baby blue yarn tail in the last front loop left on round 22 ❾.

Round of frills: skip the stitch where you attached the yarn, sc in next st, hdc inc in next st, sc in next st, (slst in next st, sc in next st, hdc inc in next st, sc in next st) repeat 15 times [79]

Slst in first st. Fasten off and weave in the yarn end ❿.

ASSEMBLY

- Flatten the arms and sew them to the body between rounds 19 and 20.
- Sew the strap around the chest and arms. Both ends should meet in the middle.
- Position and sew the hair base on top of the head ⓫. The hair base covers up to round 3 at the front of the head. At the back, the distance between the hair base and the body should be 1 round.
- Position the outer first and sixth strand symmetrically to the center of the face. Pull them backward, touching the hair base, and sew the tips to the head ⓬.
- Position strands 2, 3, 4, 5 sideways, touching the first strand. Sew the tips to the head.
- Sew the hair bun on top of the hair base. Stuff the bun with fiberfill before closing the seam ⓬.
- Sew the tiara in front of the hair bun, with the wrong side facing forward.
- Sew the body to the skirt, between rounds 4-5. Stuff the body with fiberfill before closing the seam.
- Embroider a white line around the waist, making a "V" shape at the front.
- With off-white yarn, embroider decorations on the lower part of the skirt between rounds 14-20 ⓭.

CINDERELLA IN MAID DRESS

HEAD

→ *in light peach yarn*

Repeat the pattern for Cinderella's head. Use a single strand of peach yarn to embroider the smile.

BODY

→ *start in off-white yarn*

Hold the head upside down and pull up a loop of off-white yarn in the second front loop left on round 18. Work the first stitch in the same stitch where you attached the yarn.

Rnd 19: ch 1, FLO (sc in next st, inc in next st) repeat 6 times [18]

Rnd 20: (sc in next 5 st, inc in next st) repeat 3 times [21]

Change to dark brown yarn.

Rnd 21 – 22: sc in all 21 st [21]

Rnd 23: (sc in next 6 st, inc in next st) repeat 3 times [24]

Fasten off with an invisible join, leaving a long tail for sewing ⓮.

ARM

➜ make 2, start in light peach yarn

Rnd 1: start 5 sc in a magic ring [5]
Rnd 2 – 5: sc in all 5 st [5]
Change to off-white yarn.
Rnd 6: work this round in FLO, sc in next 2 st, inc in next st, sc in next 2 st [6]
Rnd 7 – 11: sc in all 6 st [6]
Fasten off, leaving a long tail for sewing. The arms don't need to be stuffed.

HAIR

➜ in light brown yarn

Rnd 1: start 6 sc in a magic ring [6]
Rnd 2: inc in all 6 st [12]
Rnd 3: (sc in next st, inc in next st) repeat 6 times [18]
Rnd 4: (sc in next st, inc in next st, sc in next st) repeat 6 times [24]
Rnd 5: (sc in next 3 st, inc in next st) repeat 6 times [30]
Rnd 6: (sc in next 2 st, inc in next st, sc in next 2 st) repeat 6 times [36]
Rnd 7 – 9: sc in all 36 st [36]
Rnd 10: slst in next st. Continue making the hair strands:
Strand 1: ch 23, start in second ch from hook, sc in next 10 ch, hdc in next 8 ch, dc in next 4 ch,
Continue on the hair base, skip next 2 st, slst in next st,
Strand 2: ch 22, start in second ch from hook, sc in next 10 st, hdc in next 8 ch, dc in next 3 ch,
Continue on the hair base, skip next 2 st, slst in next st,
Strand 3: ch 21, start in second ch from hook, sc in next 10 ch, hdc in next 8 ch, dc in next 2 ch,
Continue on the hair base, skip next 2 st, slst in next 6 st,
Strand 4 – 8: (ch 11, start in second ch from hook, sc

in all 10 ch, continue on the hair base, slst in next st) repeat 5 times,
Strand 9: ch 11, start in second ch from hook, sc in next 8 ch, slst in next 2 ch,
Continue on the hair base, slst in next st, sc in next st,
Strand 10: ch 11, start in second ch from hook, sc in next 8 ch, slst in next 2 ch,
Continue on the hair base, slst in next st [17 + 10 strands] Leave the remaining stitch unworked.
Fasten off with an invisible join, leaving a long tail for sewing.
Flip the hair base inside out, so that the wrong side is facing outward. Hide the starting yarn tail on the inside by passing it through the magic ring ⑮.

HEAD SCARF

→ *in off-white yarn*

Crochet in rows.
Row 1: work in a magic ring: 2 sc, ch 2, 2 sc, ch 1, turn [4 + ch-2-space]
Row 2: hdc in next st, sc in next st, sc + ch 2 + sc in ch-space, sc in next st, hdc in next st, ch 1, turn [6 + ch-2-space]
Row 3: hdc inc in next st, sc in next 2 st, sc + ch 2 + sc in ch-space, sc in next 2 st, hdc inc in next st, ch 1, turn [10 + ch-2-space]
Row 4: hdc in next st, sc in next 4 st, sc + ch 2 + sc in ch-space, sc in next 4 st, hdc in next st, ch 1, turn [12 + ch-2-space]
Row 5: hdc inc in next st, sc in next 5 st, sc + ch 2 + sc in ch-space, sc in next 5 st, hdc inc in next st, ch 1, turn [16 + ch-2-space]
Row 6: hdc in next st, sc in next 7 st, sc + ch 2 + sc in ch-space, sc in next 7 st, hdc in next st, ch 1, turn [18 + ch-2-space]
Row 7: hdc inc in next st, sc in next 8 st, sc + ch 2 + sc in ch-space, sc in next 8 st, hdc inc in next st, ch 1, turn [22 + ch-2-space]
Row 8: hdc in next st, sc in next 10 st, sc + ch 2 + sc in ch-space, sc in next 10 st, hdc in next st, ch 1, turn [24 + ch-2-space]

Row 9: hdc inc in next st, sc in next 11 st, sc + ch 2 + sc in ch-space, sc in next 11 st, hdc inc in next st, ch 1, turn [28 + ch-2-space]
Row 10: hdc in next st, sc in next 13 st, sc + ch 2 + sc in ch-space, sc in next 13 st, hdc in next st, ch 1 [30 + ch-2-space] (16)
Sc in next 24 row-ends at the bottom, ch 12.
Fasten off, leaving a short yarn tail.
Pull up a loop of off-white yarn at the opposite end of the scarf (17). Leave a long starting yarn tail. Ch 12.
Fasten off, leaving a short yarn tail (18).

SKIRT

→ *start in ecru yarn*

Leave a 4" / 10 cm long starting yarn tail, this will later be used to join both Cinderellas together.
Rnd 1: start 6 sc in a magic ring [6]
Rnd 2: inc in all 6 st [12]
Rnd 3: (sc in next st, inc in next st) repeat 6 times [18]
Rnd 4: (sc in next st, inc in next st, sc in next st) repeat 6 times [24]
Rnd 5: (sc in next 3 st, inc in next st) repeat 6 times [30]
Rnd 6: (sc in next 2 st, inc in next st, sc in next 2 st) repeat 6 times [36]
Rnd 7: (sc in next 5 st, inc in next st) repeat 6 times [42]
Rnd 8: (sc in next 3 st, inc in next st, sc in next 3 st) repeat 6 times [48]
Rnd 9 – 10: sc in all 48 st [48]
Rnd 11: (sc in next 7 st, inc in next st) repeat 6 times [54]
Rnd 12 – 17: sc in all 54 st [54]
Rnd 18: (sc in next 4 st, inc in next st, sc in next 4 st) repeat 6 times [60]
Rnd 19 – 22: sc in all 60 st [60]
Rnd 23: (sc in next 9 st, inc in next st) repeat 6 times [66]
Change to off-white yarn. Don't fasten off the ecru yarn, but bring the yarn to the outside.
Rnd 24: BLO sc in all 66 st [66]
Next, we make a round of frills. Since the wrong side of the frills should face outward, you turn your crochet work, and work round 25 in BLO (19).
Rnd 25: work this round in BLO, skip 1 st, sc in next st, hdc inc in next st, sc in next st, (slst in next st, sc in next st, hdc inc in next st, sc in next st) repeat 15 times,

21 22 23 24 25 26 27 28 29 30 31

slst in next 2 st [81]
Slst in next st. Fasten off, leaving a 20" / 50 cm long yarn tail. Using a yarn needle, weave the yarn tail to the first back loop left on round 24. This tail will later be used to sew both Cinderellas together.

Pull up a loop of the ecru yarn in the last front loop left on round 23 (20). Work the first stitch in the same stitch where you attached the yarn.
Decorative round: slst in all 66 st [66]
Slst in next st. Fasten off and weave in the yarn end (21).

APRON

→ *in off-white yarn*

Leave a 32" / 80 cm long starting tail. Ch 6. Crochet in rows.
Row 1: start in second ch from hook, sc in all 5 ch, ch 1, turn [5]
Row 2: inc in next st, sc in next 3 st, inc in next st, ch 1, turn [7]
Row 3 – 4: sc in all 7 st, ch 1, turn [7]
Row 5: inc in next st, sc in next 5 st, inc in next st,

ch 1, turn [9]
Row 6: sc in all 9 st, ch 1, turn [9]
Row 7: sc in all 9 st [9]
Fasten off and weave in the yarn end.
Insert your hook in the first stitch of row 1, take the starting yarn tail on your hook and pull up a loop 22.
Finishing round: sc in all st and row-ends around the apron. Crochet an inc in each corner.
Slst in next st. Fasten off, leaving a long tail for sewing 23.

PATCH

→ *in baby blue yarn*

Rnd 1: work in a magic ring: (sc, ch 2) repeat 4 times [4 + 4 ch-space]
Tighten the magic ring. Fasten off, leaving a yarn tail.
Using a yarn needle, pass the yarn tail through the first stitch to make a square shape 24.
Split your blue yarn in strands and use a single strand to sew the patch to the apron.

ASSEMBLY

- Flatten the arms and sew them to the body between rounds 19 and 20.
- With dark brown yarn, create shoulder straps, starting at round 21, from the front to the back of the body.
- Position and sew the hair base on the head 25. At the front, the hair base covers up to round 2 of the head. At the back, the distance between the hair base and the body should be 4 rounds.
- Position the fourth and tenth strands symmetrically to the center of the face. Pull them backward, touching the hair base, and sew the tips to the head 26.
- Position strands 5, 6, 7, 8 sideways, touching the fourth strand. Position strand 9 next to tenth strand. Sew the tips to the head.
- Braid strands 1, 2 and 3 together, then drape the braid over the shoulder 27.
- Put the headscarf on top of the hair and tie the straps at the back of the neck. Secure it with a few tiny stitches to hold it in place 28.
- Sew the body to the skirt, between rounds 4-5. Stuff the body with fiberfill before closing the seam.
- Sew the apron to the skirt.

JOINING BOTH CINDERELLAS

Flip both Cinderellas inside out, so that the wrong sides of both are outward. Make a knot with the yarn tails left from the magic rings. Try to leave a small space between both pieces 29.
Flip the Cinderella in the blue gown back, so the right side is outward. Don't flip the Cinderella in ecru maid dress back, but keep her with the wrong side outward. The pieces don't need to be stuffed. Gently push the maid inside the princess 30.
With the off-white yarn tail left on the maid's skirt, sew the last rounds of both Cinderellas together, using only the back loops on both rounds for sewing 31.

PRINCE WITH CINDERELLA'S SHOE

(not reversible)

SKILL LEVEL

★★★

SIZE

4" / 10 cm tall when made with the indicated yarn.

MATERIALS

- Sport weight yarn in:
  - light peach
  - off-white
  - dark blue
  - blue
  - dark brown
  - light brown
  - peach (leftover)
- Fingering weight yarn in
  - off-white
  - pale blue

  (or you could use 1/2 of the strands of your sport weight yarn)
- B-1 / 2.25 mm crochet hook
- 2.0 mm crochet hook (for working with fingering weight yarn)
- Yarn needle
- Embroidery needle
- Stitch markers
- Fiberfill for stuffing
- Safety eyes (6mm)
- A piece of cardboard or rigid plastic sheet (1x1"/ 2x2 cm)
- Aluminum craft wire (diameter 0.5 mm, 5"/ 12 cm long)
- Scissors
- Pliers
- Optional: a small plastic bead
- Optional: yarn glue

Scan or visit
www.amigurumi.com/5307
to share pictures and find inspiration.

HEAD

→ in light peach yarn

Rnd 1: start 6 sc in a magic ring [6]
Rnd 2: inc in all 6 st [12]
Rnd 3: (sc in next st, inc in next st) repeat 6 times [18]
Rnd 4: (sc in next st, inc in next st, sc in next st) repeat 6 times [24]
Rnd 5: (sc in next 3 st, inc in next st) repeat 6 times [30]
Rnd 6 – 8: sc in all 30 st [30]
Rnd 9: (sc in next 9 st, inc in next st) repeat 3 times [33]
Rnd 10 – 14: sc in all 33 st [33]
Insert the safety eyes between rounds 11-12. The distance between the eyes should be 7 stitches. Make sure that the beginning of the round is situated at the center back.
Rnd 15: (sc in next 9 st, dec) repeat 3 times [30]
Rnd 16: (sc in next 3 st, dec) repeat 6 times [24]
Rnd 17: (sc in next 2 st, dec) repeat 6 times [18]
Rnd 18: (sc in next st, dec) repeat 6 times [12]
Stuff the head firmly with fiberfill.
Rnd 19: BLO dec 6 times [6]
Fasten off, leaving a yarn tail. Using your yarn needle, weave the yarn tail through the front loop of each remaining stitch and pull it tight to close. Weave in the yarn end.

- Embroider rosy cheeks using peach yarn, between rounds 12-13.
- Split your dark brown yarn in strands and use 2 strands to embroider a smile on round 13 and eyebrows on round 9 (1).

BODY

→ start in off-white yarn

Hold the head upside down and pull up a loop of off-white yarn in the second front loop left on round 18 (2). Work the first stitch in the same stitch where you attached the yarn.
Rnd 19: ch 1, FLO (sc in next st, inc in next st) repeat 6 times [18]
Rnd 20: (sc in next 5 st, inc in next st) repeat 3 times [21]
Rnd 21 – 25: sc in all 21 st [21]
Change to dark blue yarn.
Rnd 26 – 28: sc in all 21 st [21]
Rnd 29: (sc in next 5 st, dec) repeat 3 times [18]

Rnd 30: (sc in next st, dec) repeat 6 times [12]
Stuff the body firmly with fiberfill.
Rnd 31: dec 6 times [6]
Fasten off, leaving a yarn tail. Using your yarn needle, weave the yarn tail through the front loop of each remaining stitch and pull it tight to close. Weave in the yarn end 3.

HAIR

in light brown yarn

Rnd 1: start 6 sc in a magic ring [6]
Rnd 2: inc in all 6 st [12]
Rnd 3: (sc in next st, inc in next st) repeat 6 times [18]
Rnd 4: (sc in next st, inc in next st, sc in next st) repeat 6 times [24]
Rnd 5: (sc in next 3 st, inc in next st) repeat 6 times [30]
Rnd 6: (sc in next 2 st, inc in next st, sc in next 2 st) repeat 6 times [36]
Rnd 7 – 10: sc in all 36 st [36]
Rnd 11: slst in next st, sc in next st, hdc in next st, dc inc in next st, hdc in next st, sc in next st, slst in next 9 st, continue making the hair strands,

Strand 1: ch 9, start in second ch from hook, sc in all 8 ch, continue on the hair base, slst in next st,
Strand 2 – 5: (ch 11, start in second ch from hook, sc in all 10 ch, continue on the hair base, slst in next st) repeat 4 times,
Strand 6: ch 9, start in second ch from hook, sc in next 8 ch, continue on the hair base, slst in next 9 st, sc in next st, hdc in next st, dc inc in next st, hdc in next st, sc in next st, slst in next st [37 + 6 strands] Leave the remaining stitch unworked.
Fasten off, leaving a long tail for sewing.

Flip the hair base inside out, so that the wrong side is facing outward. Hide the starting yarn tail on the inside by passing it through the magic ring 4.

LEFT LEG (KNEELING ON GROUND)

→ *in dark blue yarn*

Rnd 1: start 6 sc in a magic ring [6]
Rnd 2: (inc in next st, 3 hdc in next st, inc in next st) repeat 2 times [14]
Continue crocheting the upper leg.
Rnd 3a: sc in next 4 st, *(mark the fourth stitch of Rnd 2 in which you made the last sc, it will be used as the starting point to make the lower leg)* 5, ch 4, skip next 6 st, sc in next 4 st [8] 6 7
Rnd 4a: sc in next 4 st, sc in next 4 ch, sc in next 4 st [12]
Rnd 5a: sc in next 4 st, hdc in next 3 st, hdc inc in next st, hdc in next 3 st, sc in next st [13]
Rnd 6a: sc in next 7 st, hdc in next 2 st, hdc inc in next st, hdc in next 2 st, sc in next st [14]
Rnd 7a: sc in next 9 st, inc in next st, sc in next 4 st [15]
Rnd 8a – 9a: sc in all 15 st [15]
Fasten off with an invisible join, leaving a long tail for sewing 8

Continue crocheting the lower leg. Pull up a loop of dark blue yarn in the marked stitch on round 2 9. Start in the same stitch where you attached the yarn.
Rnd 3b: ch 1, sc in next 8 st, hdc in next 4 ch [12] 10
Rnd 4b: sc in next 8 st, hdc in next 4 st [12]
Rnd 5b: (dec, sc in next 4 st) repeat 2 times [10]
Rnd 6b: (sc in next 3 st, dec) repeat 2 times [8]
Rnd 7b – 8b: sc in all 8 st [8]
Rnd 9b: (sc in next 2 st, dec) repeat 2 times [6]
Fasten off, leaving a yarn tail. Using your yarn needle, weave the yarn tail through the front loop of each remaining stitch and pull it tight to close 11. The leg doesn't need to be stuffed yet. Stuff it later, after attaching the boot.

RIGHT LEG

→ *in dark blue yarn*

Rnd 1: start 6 sc in a magic ring [6]
Rnd 2: (inc in next st, 3 hdc in next st, inc in next st) repeat 2 times [14]
Continue crocheting the upper leg.
Rnd 3a: sc in next 4 st, *(mark the fourth stitch of Rnd 2 in which you made the last sc, it will be used as the starting point to make the lower leg)* 5, ch 4, skip next 6 st, sc in next 4 st [8] 6 7
Rnd 4a: sc in next 4 st, sc in next 4 ch, sc in next 4 st [12]
Rnd 5a: sc in next 3 st, hdc in next st, hdc inc in next st, hdc in next 3 st, sc in next 4 st [13]

Rnd 6a: sc in next 4 st, hdc in next st, hdc inc in next st, hdc in next 3 st, sc in next 4 st [14]
Rnd 7a: slst in next 3 st, sc in next st, hdc in next 2 st, hdc inc in next st, hdc in next st, sc in next st, slst in next 5 st [15]
Fasten off, leaving a long tail for sewing 12.

Continue crocheting the lower leg. Pull up a loop of dark blue yarn in the marked stitch on round 2 13. Start in the same stitch where you attached the yarn.
Rnd 3b: ch 1, sc in next 8 st, hdc in next 4 ch [12]
Rnd 4b: sc in next 8 st, hdc in next 4 st [12]
Rnd 5b: (dec, sc in next 4 st) repeat 2 times [10]
Rnd 6b: (sc in next 3 st, dec) repeat 2 times [8]
Rnd 7b – 8b: sc in all 8 st [8]
Rnd 9b: (sc in next 2 st, dec) repeat 2 times [6]
Fasten off, leaving a yarn tail. Using your yarn needle, weave the yarn tail through the front loop of each remaining stitch and pull it tight to close 14.
The leg doesn't need to be stuffed yet. Stuff it later, after attaching the boot.

BOOT

→ *make 2, start in dark brown yarn*

Note: *Crochet the boots with a relaxed tension to leave enough space for inserting the lower legs afterward.*
Ch 5. Stitches are worked around both sides of the foundation chain.
Rnd 1: start in second ch from hook, sc in next 3 ch, 4 sc in next ch. Continue on the other side of the foundation chain, sc in next 2 ch, inc in next ch [11]
Rnd 2: inc in next st, sc in next 2 st, inc in next 4 st, sc in next 2 st, inc in next 2 st [18]
Prepare a piece of cardboard or rigid plastic sheet, cut to match the shape of the sole but slightly smaller. This will be inserted into the bottom of the boot for added support.
Rnd 3: BLO sc in all 18 st [18]
Rnd 4: sc in next 4 st, dec 4 times, sc in next 4 st, dec [13]
Insert the cardboard/rigid plastic sheet 15.
Rnd 5: sc in next 4 st, dec 2 times, sc in next 5 st [11]
Rnd 6: sc in next 4 st, dec, sc in next 5 st [10]
Stuff only the tip of the boot lightly with fiberfill.

Rnd 7: sc in next 4 st, inc in next st, sc in next 5 st [11]
Rnd 8: sc in next 10 st, inc in next st [12]
Rnd 9 – 10: sc in all 12 st [12]
Change to light brown yarn. Leave a long dark brown yarn tail for sewing.
Rnd 11: slst in all 12 st [12]
Fasten off with an invisible join and weave in the yarn end.
Carefully insert the legs into the boots, as this step is essential for the doll to stand on its own. If the leg doesn't go in deep enough, the leg will end up being too long. The bottom of the leg should reach the bottom of the boot, and the top part of the boot should cover round 5 of the leg. Sew the boot to the leg using the dark brown yarn tail of the boot 16.

JACKET

→ *in blue yarn*

Ch 7. Crochet in rows.
Row 1: start in second ch from hook, sc in next 5 ch, inc in next ch, ch 1, turn [7]
Row 2: inc in next st, sc in next 6 st, ch 3, turn [8]
Row 3: start in third ch from hook, sc in this ch, sc in next 7 st, inc in next st, ch 1, turn [10]
Row 4: sc in all 10 st, ch 1, turn [10]
Row 5: sc in next 7 st, hdc in next 2 st, hdc inc in next st, ch 1, turn [11]
Row 6: hdc in next 4 st, sc in next 7 st, ch 1, turn [11]
Row 7: sc in next 7 st, hdc in next 3 st, hdc inc in next st, ch 1, turn [12]
Row 8: hdc in next 5 st, sc in next 7 st, ch 1, turn [12]
Row 9: sc in next 7 st, hdc in next 4 st, hdc inc in next st, ch 1, turn [13]
Row 10: inc in next st, sc in next 12 st, ch 1, turn [14]
Row 11: sc in next 13 st, inc in next st, ch 1, turn [15]
Row 12: slst in next 4 st, ch 5, start in second ch from hook, sc in next 4 ch, skip the stitch where the last slst was made, sc in next 11 st, ch 1, turn [19]
Row 13: sc in next 13 st, dec, ch 1, turn [14]
Row 14: dec, sc in next 12 st, ch 1, turn [13]
Row 15: sc in next 7 st, hdc in next 4 st, hdc2tog, ch 1, turn [12]
Row 16: hdc in next 5 st, sc in next 7 st, ch 1, turn [12]

Row 17: sc in next 7 st, hdc in next 3 st, hdc2tog, ch 1, turn [11]
Row 18: hdc in next 4 st, sc in next 7 st, ch 1, turn [11]
Row 19: sc in next 7 st, hdc in next 2 st, hdc2tog, ch 1, turn [10]
Row 20: sc in all 10 st, ch 1, turn [10]
Row 21: sc in next 8 st, dec, ch 1, turn [9]
Row 22: dec, sc in next 6 st, ch 1, turn [7] Leave the remaining stitch unworked.
Row 23: sc in next 5 st, dec [6]
Fasten off, leaving a long tail for sewing 17.

ARM

→ *make 2, start in light peach yarn*

Rnd 1: start 6 sc in a magic ring [6]
Rnd 2: sc in all 6 st [6]
Change to off-white yarn.
Rnd 3: sc in next 2 st, inc in next st, sc in next 3 st [7]
Rnd 4: sc in all 7 st [7]
Change to blue yarn.
Rnd 5: sc in next 6 st, inc in next st [8]
Rnd 6 – 7: sc in all 8 st [8]

Pause but don't fasten off the blue yarn.
Pull up a loop of light brown yarn between rounds 4-5 and make 7 surface slip stitches around (18).
Continue crocheting the arm with the blue yarn.
Rnd 8: FPsc in next 3 st, hdc in next 5 st [8]
Rnd 9 – 12: sc in all 8 st [8]
Fasten off, leaving a long tail for sewing. The arm doesn't need to be stuffed. Using your yarn needle, weave the yarn tail through the front loop of each remaining stitch and pull it tight to close.

EPAULETS

→ *make 2, in light brown yarn*

Rnd 1: start sc + hdc + 2 dc + hdc + sc in a magic ring [6]
Tighten the magic ring. Fasten off, leaving a long tail for sewing.

RUFFLE

→ *in fingering weight off-white yarn*

Note: *It's recommended to use thinner yarn and a smaller hook size. You could also choose to split your sport weight yarn and use only half of the strands.*
Ch 5. Crochet in rows.
Row 1: start in third ch from hook, (dc + 2 ch + dc inc + 2 ch in next ch) repeat 3 times, slst in last ch.
Fasten off, leaving a long tail for sewing (19).
Pinch and sew through the foundation chain to turn it into a ruffled shape (20) (21).

CINDERELLA'S SHOE

→ *in fingering weight pale blue yarn*

Note: *It's recommended to use thinner yarn and a smaller hook size. You could also choose to split your sport weight yarn and use only half of the strands.*
Ch 8. Stitches are worked around both sides of the foundation chain.
Rnd 1: start in second ch from hook, sc in next 6 ch, 3 sc in next ch. Continue on the other side of the foundation chain, sc in next 5 ch, inc in next ch [16]
Note: *In round 2 we add aluminum wire to the crochet work for strength. If you're crocheting for small children, please leave out the wire and omit making the heel.*
Rnd 2: take a piece of aluminum wire and crochet over the wire (22): sc in next 7 st (23), 3 sc in next st, sc in next 8 st, unite both ends of the wire in front of you (24), and pass your crochet hook over both ends to the other side (25), inc in the same st where the last st is made [20]
Twist both ends of the wire into one and bend the tip (26).
Rnd 3: BLO sc in all 20 st [20]
Rnd 4: sc in next 5 st, dec, sc3tog, dec, sc in next 6 st, dec [15]
Rnd 5: slst in next 5 st, sc3tog, slst in next 7 st [13]
Fasten off with an invisible join, leaving a long yarn tail (27). With the yarn tail, wrap the twisted wire tightly to make the high heel. Weave in the yarn end.
Optional: Glue a plastic bead to the front of the shoe (28).

ASSEMBLY

- Position the hair base onto the head. Make sure that strands 1-6 are positioned symmetrically to the center of the face (29). Sew the hair base on.
- Fold strand 1 and strand 6 backward, following the shape of the hair base. Sew the tips to the face (30).
- Curl strand 2 over strand 1. Curl strand 3-5 in the direction of strand 6. Sew the tips to fix the positions.
- Sew the legs to the bottom of the body in kneeling position. The left knee should touch the ground. This is a crucial step to make sure the prince can stand independently.
  Note: *If he cannot stand properly, it might be caused by the left thigh being shorter than the right lower leg. You can try to bend the right knee more and raise the position of that knee.*
- Sew the jacket to the body, leaving a gap with a width of 2-3 stitches at the front of the body (31).
- Sew the ruffle to the neck seam, centered on the jacket gap.
- Sew the arms onto the jacket. Don't sew them too high up, as we still need to attach the epaulets on the shoulders. Position the arms slightly diagonally, so they can be raised towards the middle (32).
- Sew the epaulets on the shoulders.
- With light brown yarn, embroider 2 pairs of French knots on the jacket as buttons (32).
- Sew or glue Cinderella's shoe to the hands.

REVERSIBLE ROSE FAIRY

SKILL LEVEL

SIZE

4" / 10 cm tall when made with the indicated yarn.

MATERIALS

- Sport weight yarn in:
  - dark red
  - red
  - bright red
  - green
  - light peach
  - light pink
  - black (leftover)
- B-1 / 2.0 mm crochet hook
- Yarn needle
- Embroidery needle
- Stitch marker
- Fiberfill for stuffing
- Optional: flower wire (gauge #22, 3"/8 cm long)
- Optional: pliers

Scan or visit www.amigurumi.com/5308 to share pictures and find inspiration.

HEAD ①

→ *start in dark red yarn*

Rnd 1: start 6 sc in a magic ring [6]
Rnd 2: inc in next 3 st, BLO inc in next st, continue working in both loops, inc in next 2 st [12]
Rnd 3: (sc in next st, inc in next st) repeat 4 times, BLO (sc in next st, inc in next st) repeat 2 times [18]
Rnd 4: start working in BLO, (sc in next st, inc in next st, sc in next st) repeat 3 times, sc in next st, inc in next st, mark the remaining front loop on Rnd 3 below the previous inc *(green marker ②)*, continue working in both loops, sc in next st, (sc in next st, inc in next st, sc in next st) repeat 2 times [24] ③
Rnd 5: sc in next 2 st, continue working in BLO, sc in next st, inc in next st, continue working in both loops, sc in next 3 st, inc in next st, sc in next 3 st, continue working in BLO, inc in next st, (sc in next 3 st, inc in next st) repeat 3 times [30]
Continue working with 2 colors, alternating light peach and dark red yarn. The color change is indicated in italics.
Note: *I use the cut-and-tie technique (p. 17). It's a bit time-consuming, but limits tension issues or colors popping through.*
Rnd 6: *(dark red)* BLO sc in next 3 st, mark the remaining front loop on Rnd 5 below the previous sc *(blue marker ④)*, continue working in both loops, sc in next st, inc in next st, continue working in BLO, sc in next 4 st, inc in next st, sc in next 3 st, *(light peach)* sc in next st, inc in next st, sc in next st, mark the remaining front loop on Rnd 5 below the previous sc *(orange marker ⑤)*, continue working in both loops, sc in next 2 st, *(dark red)* sc in next st, inc in next st, (sc in next 4 st, inc in next st) repeat 2 times [36]
Rnd 7: *(dark red)* sc in next 14 st, *(light peach)* sc in next 8 st, *(dark red)* sc in next 14 st [36]
Rnd 8: *(dark red)* sc in next 13 st, *(light peach)* sc in next 10 st, *(dark red)* sc in next 13 st [36]
Rnd 9 – 12: *(dark red)* sc in next 13 st, *(light peach)* sc in next 11 st, *(dark red)* sc in next 12 st [36]
Rnd 13: *(dark red)* (sc in next 4 st, dec) repeat 2 times, sc in next 2 st, *(light peach)* sc in next 2 st, dec, sc in next 4 st, dec, *(dark red)* (sc in next 4 st, dec) repeat 2 times [30]
Rnd 14: *(dark red)* (sc in next 3 st, dec) repeat 2 times, sc in next 2 st, *(light peach)* sc in next st, dec, sc in next 3 st, dec, *(dark red)* (sc in next 3 st, dec) repeat 2 times [24]

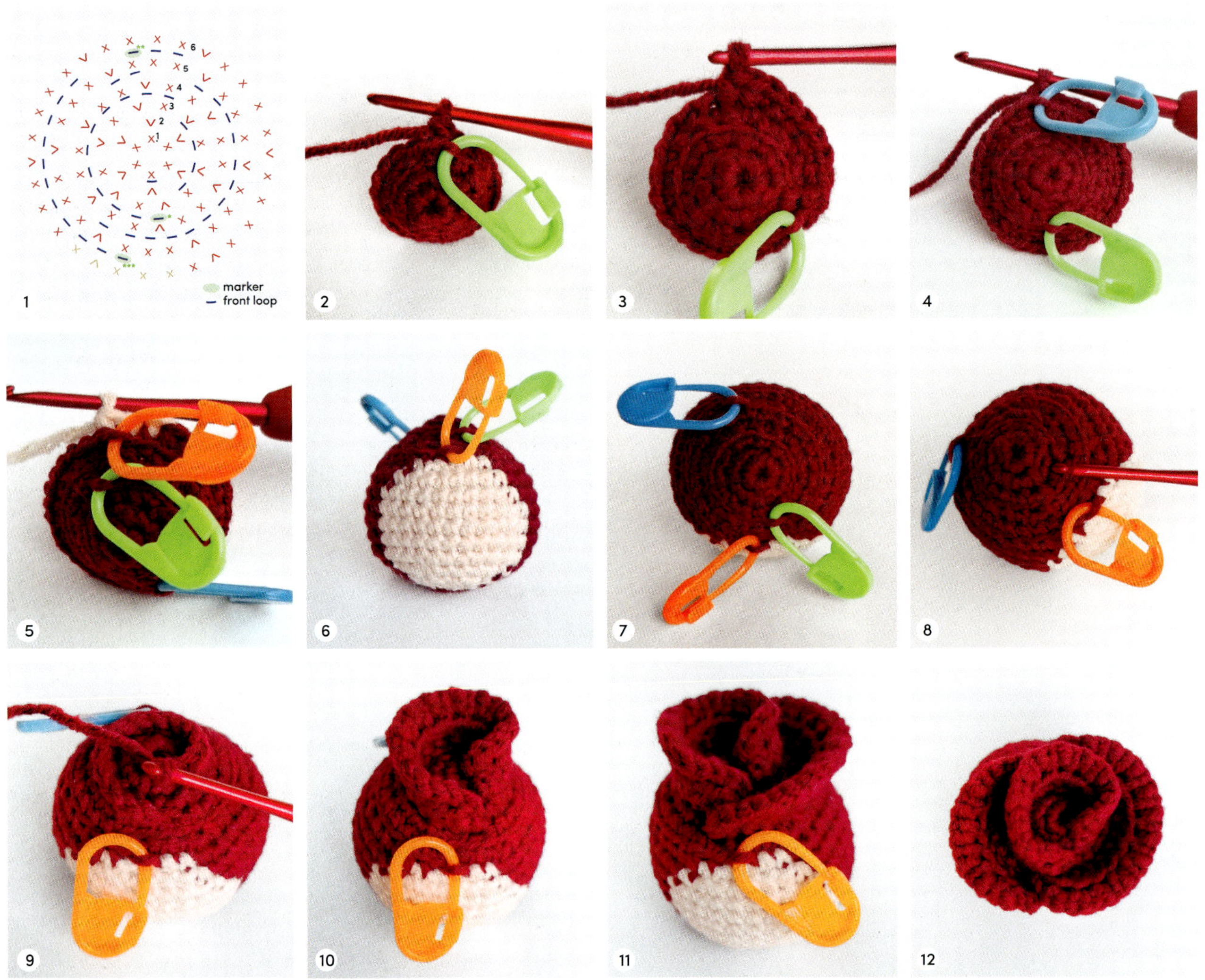

Rnd 15: *(dark red)* (sc in next 2 st, dec) repeat 2 times, sc in next 2 st, *(light peach)* dec, sc in next 2 st, dec, *(dark red)* (sc in next 2 st, dec) repeat 2 times [18]
Continue working in dark red yarn.
Rnd 16: (sc in next st, dec) repeat 6 times [12]
Stuff the head firmly with fiberfill.
Rnd 17: BLO dec 6 times [6]
Fasten off, leaving a yarn tail. Using your yarn needle, weave the yarn tail through the front loop of each remaining stitch and pull it tight to close. Weave in the yarn end (6).

PETALS ON HEAD

Next, we make 3 petals on top of the head. Hold the head upward, with the last round facing you (7). Pull up a loop of dark red yarn in a marked stitch to start a new petal.

PETAL 1

→ *in dark red yarn*

Crochet in rows. Pull up a loop of dark red yarn in the first marked stitch *(green marker)* (8).

Row 1: skip the stitch where you attached the yarn, sc in next 10 remaining front loops on Rnd 3, continue working in the front loops left on Rnd 2, sc in next 4 st, continue working in the front loop left on Rnd 1, slst in this st, ch 1, turn [15] 9
Row 2: skip 1 st, sc in next st, hdc in next 12 st, sc in next st, ch 1, turn [14]
Row 3: work this row in FLO, skip 1 st, slst in next st, inc in next 11 st, slst in next st [24]
Fasten off, leaving a yarn tail. Using your yarn needle, pass the yarn tail through the magic ring, pull tight and weave in the yarn end 10.

PETAL 2

→ *in dark red yarn*

Crochet in rows. Pull up a loop of dark red yarn in the second marked stitch *(blue marker)*.
Row 1: skip the stitch where you attached the yarn, sc in next 2 remaining front loops on Rnd 5, continue working in the front loops left on Rnd 4, sc in next 12 st, slst in next st, ch 1, turn [15]
Row 2: skip 1 st, sc in next st, hdc in next 12 st, sc in next st, ch 1, turn [14]
Row 3: work this row in FLO, skip 1 st, slst in next st, inc in next 11 st, slst in next st [24]
Fasten off and weave in the yarn end 11.

PETAL 3

→ *in dark red yarn*

Crochet in rows. Pull up a loop of dark red yarn in the third marked stitch *(orange marker)*.
Row 1: skip the stitch where you attached the yarn, sc in next 10 remaining front loops on Rnd 5, continue working in the front loops left on Rnd 4, sc in next st, slst in next st, ch 1, turn [12]
Row 2: skip 1 st, sc in next st, hdc in next 9 st, sc in next st, ch 1, turn [11]
Row 3: work this row in FLO, skip 1 st, slst in next st, inc in next 8 st, slst in next st [18]
Fasten off and weave in the yarn end 12.

HAIR STRAND

→ *in dark red yarn*

Ch 20. Crochet in rows.
Row 1: start in second ch from hook, slst in this ch, sc in next 13 ch, hdc in next 3 ch, dc in next 2 ch [19]
Fasten off, leaving a long tail for sewing.
Sew the hair strand to the right side of the face (based on the fairy's viewpoint), below the third petal, with the right side facing outward 13.

BODY AND STEM

→ *start in light peach yarn*

Hold the head upside down and pull up a loop of light peach yarn in the second front loop left on round 16 of the head 14. Work the first stitch in the same stitch where you attached the yarn.
Rnd 17: ch 1, FLO (sc in next st, inc in next st) repeat 6 times [18]
Change to red yarn.

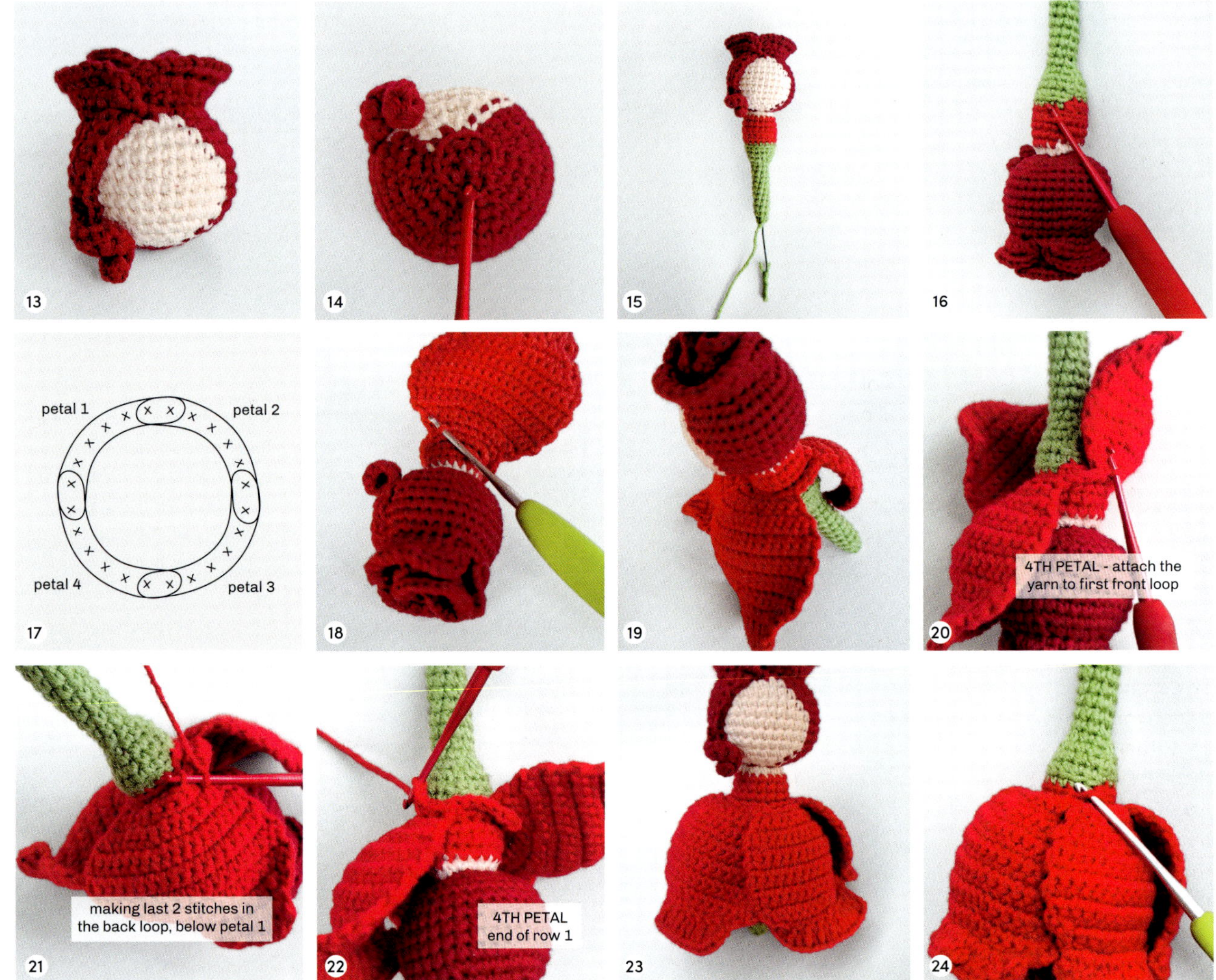

Rnd 18 – 20: sc in all 18 st [18]
Rnd 21: BLO sc in all 18 st [18]
Change to green yarn.
Rnd 22 – 23: BLO sc in all 18 st [18]
Stuff the body with fiberfill and continue stuffing the stem as you go.
Rnd 24: (sc in next 4 st, dec) repeat 3 times [15]
Rnd 25: (sc in next 3 st, dec) repeat 3 times [12]
Rnd 26: (sc in next 2 st, dec) repeat 3 times [9]
Rnd 27 – 35: sc in all 9 st [9]
Rnd 36: (sc in next st, dec) repeat 3 times [6]

Fasten off, leaving a yarn tail.
Optional: *To make the stem sturdier and bendable, you can insert wire into it. Take a piece of wire and bend one end into an eyelet. Cut the wire to the length of the stem + 1 cm. Wrap the bent end with yarn, then carefully insert the wire into the stem* 15.
Using your yarn needle, weave the yarn tail through the front loop of each remaining stitch and pull it tight to close. Weave in the yarn end.

Next, we make 9 petals on the stem — 4 upper petals and 5 lower petals.
Note: *The petals on the stem are the reversible part of this amigurumi, so it's recommended to use regular decreases. An invisible decrease is worked in the front loops only. As both sides of the final work will be visible, I prefer using a regular decrease (sc2tog), worked through both loops.*

UPPER PETALS

→ *in red yarn*

Start by making a base round. Hold the fairy upside down. Pull up a loop of red yarn in the first leftover front loop on round 20 of the body 16. Work the first stitch in the same stitch where you attached the yarn.
Rnd 21: ch 1, FLO (sc in next st, inc in next st, sc in next st) repeat 6 times [24]
Continue making a petal.

Petal 1: Continue working in rows.
Row 1: continue working in FLO, inc in next st, sc in next st, continue working in both loops, sc in next 4 st, continue working in BLO, sc in next st, inc in next st, ch 1, turn [10]
Row 2: sc in all 10 st, ch 1, turn [10]
Row 3: inc in next st, (sc in next 2 st, inc in next st) repeat 3 times, ch 1, turn [14]
Row 4: inc in next st, sc in next st, (sc in next 3 st, inc in next st) repeat 3 times, ch 1, turn [18]
Row 5 – 11: sc in all 18 st, ch 1, turn [18]
Row 12: sc2tog, (sc in next 6 st, sc2tog) repeat 2 times, ch 1, turn [15]
Row 13: sc2tog, sc in next 11 st, sc2tog, ch 1, turn [13]
Row 14: sc2tog, sc in next 3 st, sc2tog, sc in next 4 st, sc2tog, ch 1, turn [10]
Row 15: hdc inc in next st, dc inc in next 8 st, hdc inc in next st [20]
Fasten off and weave in the yarn ends.
Note: *When folded up, the tip of the upper petal should nearly reach the tip of the petals on the head. If your petal is shorter (due to working with a different tension), you can adjust by adding one or more sc rows after working row 11 or by sizing up your crochet hook.*

We continue crocheting the other petals - the base round needs to fit 4 petals in total. This will work out, as some stitches of the first row will be overlapping the stitches of the adjacent petal 17.

Petal 2: Pull up a loop of red yarn in the first front loop left on row 1 of the first petal (you worked the last 2 stitches in back loops only) 18.
Ch 1. Work the first stitch in the same stitch where you joined the yarn.
Repeat Rows 1-15 of petal 1.
Fasten off and weave in the yarn ends.

Petal 3: Pull up a loop of red yarn in the first front loop left on row 1 of the second petal.
Ch 1. Work the first stitch in the same stitch where you joined the yarn.
Repeat Rows 1-15 of petal 1.
Fasten off and weave in the yarn ends.

Petal 4: After making three petals, you will notice that there are only 4 stitches remaining on the base round and 2 front loops of the adjacent petal 19. However, you'll need 8 stitches to make the last petal. The last 2 stitches of row 1 should therefore be worked below the first petal. Since you started the first row of the first petal working in front loops only, you'll have the remaining back loops available for the fourth petal 20 21 22 23.
Pull up a loop of red yarn in the first front loop left on row 1 of the third petal. Ch 1. Work the first stitch in the same stitch where you joined the yarn.
Repeat Rows 1-15 of petal 1.
Fasten off and weave in the yarn ends

LOWER PETALS

→ *in bright red yarn*

Start by making a base round. Hold the fairy upside down. Pull up a loop of bright red yarn in the first leftover front loop on round 21 of the body 24. Work the first stitch in the same stitch where you attached the yarn. Leave a 6"/15 cm starting yarn tail.
Rnd 22: ch 1, FLO (sc in next st, inc in next st, sc in next st) repeat 6 times [24]

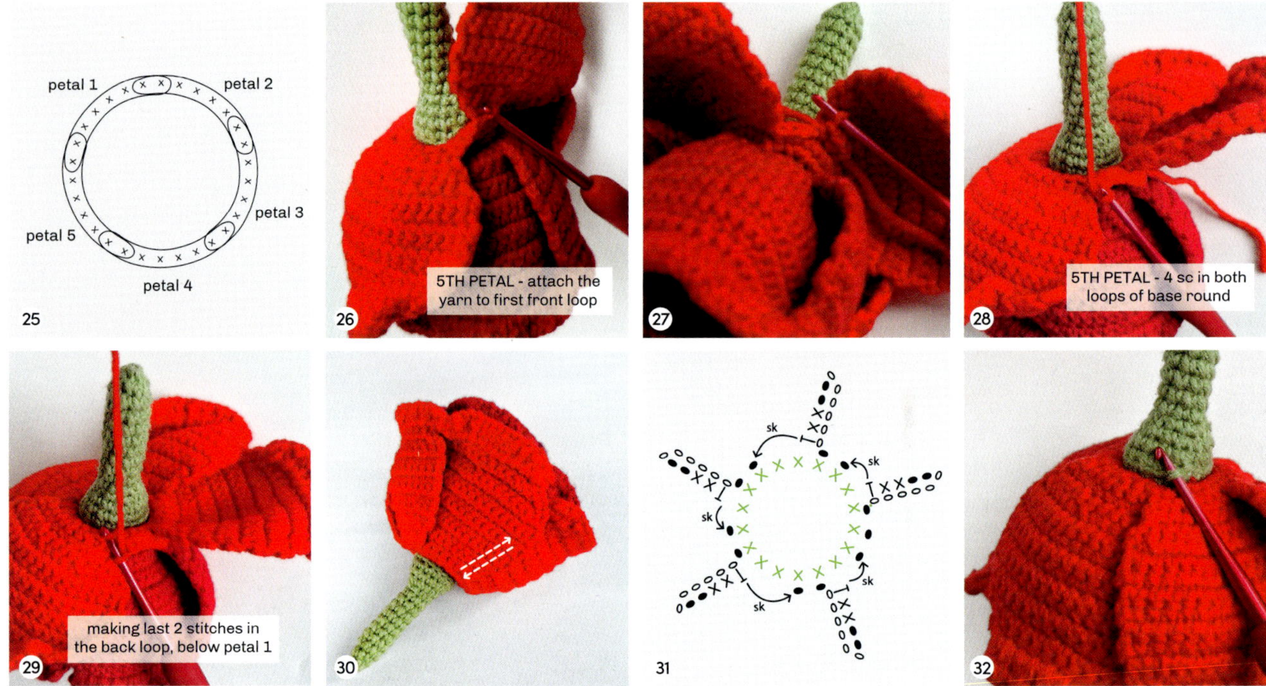

Rnd 23: (sc in next 3 st, inc in next st) repeat 6 times [30]
Continue making a petal.

Petal 1: Continue working in rows.
Row 1: continue working in FLO, inc in next st, sc in next st, continue working in both loops, sc in next 4 st, continue working in BLO, sc in next st, inc in next st, ch 1, turn [10]
Row 2: sc in all 10 st, ch 1, turn [10]
Row 3: inc in next st, (sc in next 2 st, inc in next st) repeat 3 times, ch 1, turn [14]
Row 4: inc in next st, sc in next st, (sc in next 3 st, inc in next st) repeat 3 times, ch 1, turn [18]
Row 5 – 11: sc in all 18 st, ch 1, turn [18]
Row 12: sc2tog, (sc in next 6 st, sc2tog) repeat 2 times, ch 1, turn [15]
Row 13: sc2tog, sc in next 11 st, sc2tog, ch 1, turn [13]
Row 14: sc2tog, sc in next 3 st, sc2tog, sc in next 4 st, dec, ch 1, turn [10]
Row 15: hdc inc in next st, dc inc in next 8 st, hdc inc in next st [20]
Fasten off and weave in the last yarn end.

Note: *You can adjust the length of the lower petal by adding extra rows of sc stitches after row 11. The lower petals should have the same length as the upper petals.*
Continue crocheting the other petals — the base round needs to fit 5 petals in total. This will work out, as some stitches of the first row will be overlapping the stitches of the adjacent petal 25.

Petal 2, 3 and 4: Pull up a loop of bright red yarn in the first leftover front loop of row 1 of the previous petal. Leave a 6" / 15 cm starting yarn tail. Ch 1. Work the first stitch in the same stitch where you joined the yarn. Repeat Rows 1-15 of petal 1.
Fasten off and weave in the yarn ends.

Petal 5: After making 4 petals, you will notice that there are only 4 stitches remaining on the base round and 2 front loops of the adjacent petal. However, you'll need 8 stitches to make the last petal. The last 2 stitches of row 1 should therefore be worked below the first petal. Since you started the first row of the first petal working

33

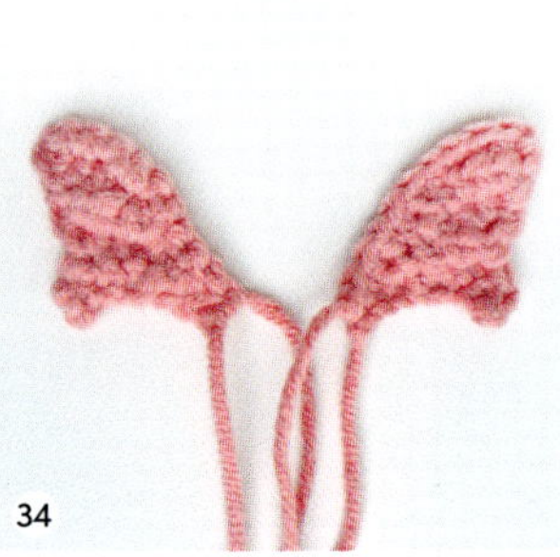
34

35

36

in front loops only, you'll have the remaining back loops available for the fifth petal.
Pull up a loop of bright red yarn in the first leftover front loop available on the fourth petal 26. Leave a 6" / 15 cm starting yarn tail. Ch 1. Work the first stitch in the same stitch where you joined the yarn.
Repeat Rows 1-15 of petal 1.
Fasten off and weave in the yarn ends 26 27 28 29.

Sew row 1 to 7 of each of the lower petals to the adjacent petal, using the starting yarn tail 30.
You don't need to sew the upper petals.

SEPALS 31

→ *in green yarn*

Hold the fairy upside down. Pull up a loop of green yarn in the first leftover front loop on round 22 of the body 32.
Rnd 23: work this round in FLO, (ch 6, start in second ch from hook, slst in next 2 ch, sc in next 2 ch, hdc in next ch, skip next st on the body, slst in next 2 st, ch 6, start in second ch from hook, slst in next 2 ch, sc in next 2 ch, hdc in next ch, skip next 2 st on the body, slst in next 2 st) repeat 2 times, ch 6, start in second ch from hook, slst in next 2 ch, sc in next 2 ch, hdc in next ch, skip next st on the body, slst in next 2 st [5 sepals]
Slst in the first front loop where you started making the sepals.
Fasten off and weave in the yarn ends 33.

WING

→ *make 2, in light pink yarn*

Ch 7. Crochet in rows.
Row 1: start in second ch from hook, sc in this ch, inc in next 2 ch, slst in next ch, ch 1, turn [6] Leave the remaining chains unworked.
Row 2: skip 1 st, slst in next st, sc in next st, hdc inc in next st, ch 1, turn [4] Leave the remaining stitches unworked.
Row 3: hdc inc in next st, sc in next st, slst in next st, ch 1, turn [4] Leave the remaining stitch unworked.
Row 4: skip 1 st, slst in next st, sc in next st, 3 hdc in next st, ch 1, turn [5]
Row 5: sc in all 5 st [5]
Sc in next 4 row-ends until you reach the first unworked ch of row 1, slst in this ch.
Fasten off, leaving a long tail for sewing 34.

LEAF

→ *in green yarn*

Ch 14. Stitches are worked around both sides of the foundation chain.
Rnd 1: start in second ch from hook, sc in next 3 ch, dc in next ch, tr in next ch, dtr in next 5 ch, tr in next ch, dc + hdc in next ch, sc + ch-2-picot + sc in next st. Continue on the other side of the foundation chain, hdc + dc in next ch, tr in next ch, dtr in next 5 ch, tr in next ch, dc in next ch, sc in next 3 ch [27]
Fasten off, leaving a long tail for sewing 35.

ARM

→ *make 2, in light peach yarn*

Rnd 1: start 5 sc in a magic ring [5]
Rnd 2 – 10: sc in all 5 st [5]
Fasten off, leaving a long tail for sewing. The arms don't need to be stuffed.

ASSEMBLY

- Flatten the arms and sew them to the body, between rounds 17-18.
- Sew the wings to the back of the body, 2 stitches apart 36.
- Sew the leaf over the last 4 rounds of the stem. Position the right side of the leaf facing upward.

EMBROIDERY ON FACE

- Embroider bangs on the left side of the face between rounds 6-10, using dark red yarn.
- Embroider eyes over round 10, about 5 stitches apart, using black yarn.
- Split your black yarn in strands and use a single strand to embroider eyelashes over round 10.
- Split your red yarn in strands and use a single strand to embroider a smile over round 11.
- Embroider rosy cheeks between rounds 10-11, 1 stitch wide, using light pink yarn.

TIP: *When you flip the fairy to the flower side, wrap the arms in front of her body to avoid the arms being raised up, so that they are hidden well inside the petals.*
TIP: *Gently fold the top edges of the petals outward for an elegant effect.*

REVERSIBLE GOLDILOCKS & BEARS

SKILL LEVEL

★☆☆

SIZE

4.5" / 11.5 cm tall (doll side)
or 2.75" / 7 cm tall (bear side)
when made with the indicated yarn.

MATERIALS

- Sport weight yarn in:
  - light peach
  - tan
  - off-white
  - yellow
  - light yellow
  - peach
  - dark brown
  - light brown
  - cream
  - black (leftover)
- B-1 / 2.25 mm crochet hook
- Safety eyes (6 mm)
- Yarn needle
- Embroidery needle
- Stitch markers
- Scissors
- Fiberfill for stuffing

Scan or visit www.amigurumi.com/5309 to share pictures and find inspiration.

***Note:** For this type of reversible amigurumi, it's recommended to crochet the stitches a bit more loosely. I use a 2.25 mm crochet hook here instead of a 2 mm crochet hook. By sizing up my crochet hook, I can achieve a more relaxed tension, making it easier to flip the characters at the end.*

GOLDILOCKS

HEAD

→ *in light peach yarn*

Rnd 1: start 6 sc in a magic ring [6]
Rnd 2: inc in all 6 st [12]
Rnd 3: (sc in next st, inc in next st) repeat 6 times [18]
Rnd 4: (sc in next st, inc in next st, sc in next st) repeat 6 times [24]
Rnd 5: (sc in next 3 st, inc in next st) repeat 6 times [30]
Rnd 6 – 8: sc in all 30 st [30]
Rnd 9: (sc in next 9 st, inc in next st) repeat 3 times [33]
Rnd 10 – 14: sc in all 33 st [33]
Insert the safety eyes between rounds 11-12. The distance between the eyes should be 7 stitches (1). Make sure that the beginning of the round is situated at the center back.
Rnd 15: (sc in next 9 st, dec) repeat 3 times [30]
Rnd 16: (sc in next 3 st, dec) repeat 6 times [24]
Rnd 17: (sc in next 2 st, dec) repeat 6 times [18]
Rnd 18: (sc in next st, dec) repeat 6 times [12]
Stuff the head firmly with fiberfill.
Rnd 19: BLO dec 6 times [6]
Fasten off, leaving a yarn tail. Using your yarn needle, weave the yarn tail through the front loop of each remaining stitch and pull it tight to close. Weave in the yarn end.

- Using peach yarn, embroider rosy cheeks between rounds 12-13.
- Split your peach yarn in strands and use a single strand to embroider a smile on round 13 (2).

BODY

→ *start in light peach yarn*

Hold the head upside down and pull up a loop of light peach yarn in the second front loop left on round 18 (3). Work the first stitch in the same stitch where you attached the yarn.
Rnd 19: ch 1, FLO (sc in next st, inc in next st) repeat 6 times [18]
Change to off-white yarn.
Rnd 20: (sc in next 5 st, inc in next st) repeat 3 times [21]
Change to light yellow yarn.
Rnd 21 – 22: sc in all 21 st [21]

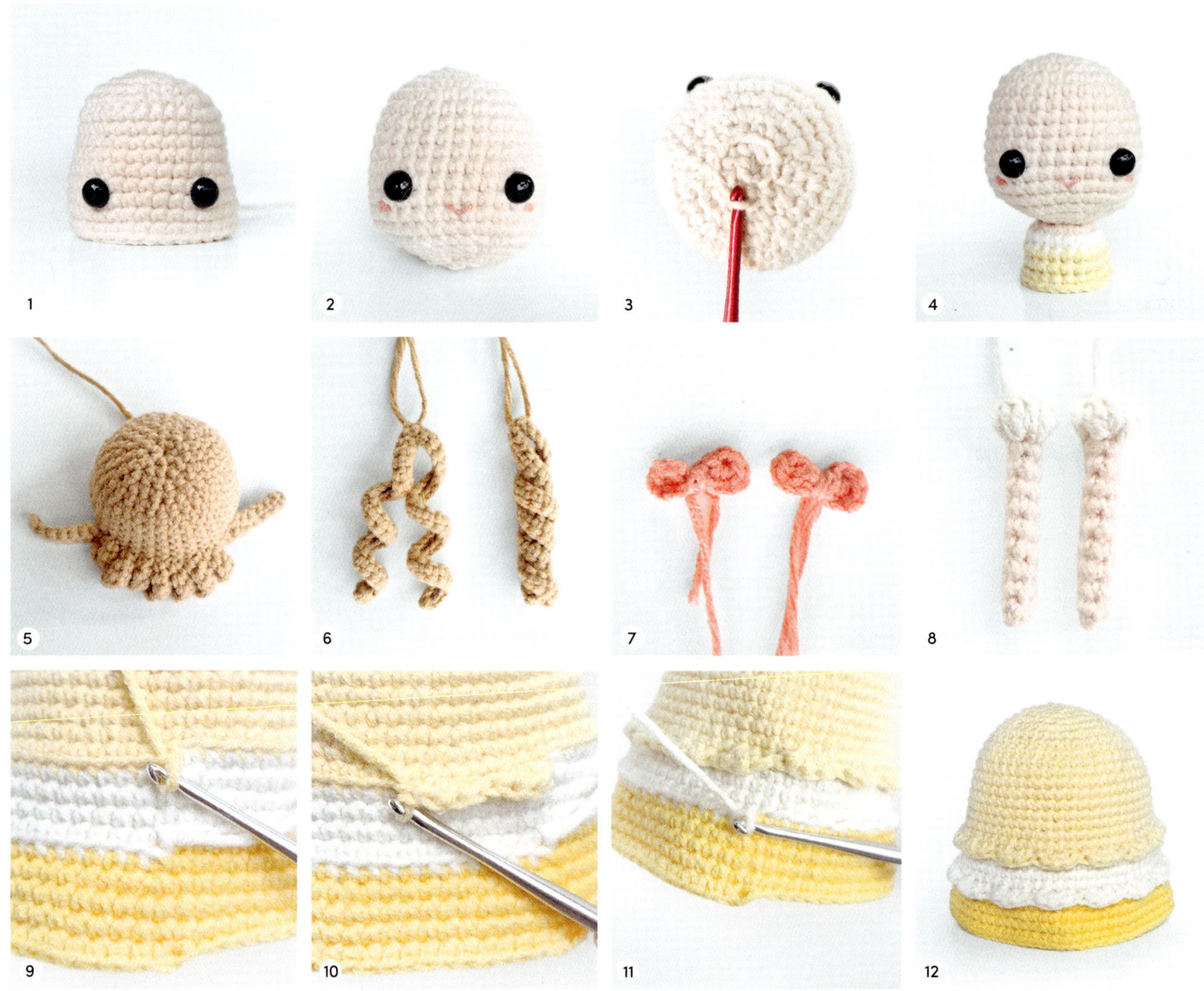

Rnd 23: (sc in next 6 st, inc in next st) repeat 3 times [24]
Fasten off, leaving a long tail for sewing 4.

HAIR

→ *in tan yarn*

Rnd 1: start 6 sc in a magic ring [6]
Rnd 2: inc in all 6 st [12]
Rnd 3: (sc in next st, inc in next st) repeat 6 times [18]
Rnd 4: (sc in next st, inc in next st, sc in next st) repeat 6 times [24]
Rnd 5: (sc in next 3 st, inc in next st) repeat 6 times [30]
Rnd 6: (sc in next 2 st, inc in next st, sc in next 2 st) repeat 6 times [36]
Rnd 7 – 10: sc in all 36 st [36]
Rnd 11: sc in next 12 st. Continue making the hair strands,
Strand 1: ch 8, start in second ch from hook, sc in next 5 ch, hdc in next ch, dc inc in next ch, continue working on the hair base, skip next 2 st, slst in next st,
Strand 2 – 8: (ch 6, start in second ch from hook, sc in all 5 ch, continue working on the hair base, slst in next st) repeat 7 times,

Strand 9: ch 11, start in second ch from hook, sc in next 7 ch, slst in next ch, skip next 2 ch, continue working on the hair base, slst in next st, sc in next 13 st.
Fasten off, leaving a long tail for sewing. Flip the hair base inside out, so that the wrong side is facing outward. Hide the starting yarn tail on the inside by passing it through the magic ring 5.

PIGTAIL

→ *make 2, in tan yarn*

Rnd 1: start in a magic ring: (ch 31, start in second ch from hook, sc in all 30 ch, slst in the magic ring) repeat 2 times.
Tighten the magic ring. Fasten off, leaving a long tail for sewing. Twist the hair strands together 6.

HAIR RIBBON

→ *make 2, in peach yarn*

Rnd 1: start in a magic ring: (ch 3, dc in the magic ring, ch 3, slst in the magic ring) repeat 2 times.
Tighten the magic ring. Fasten off, leaving a long tail for sewing. Wrap the ending yarn tail around the center of the bow and make a knot to keep it in shape 7. Leave a long tail for sewing.

ARM

→ *make 2, start in light peach yarn*

Rnd 1: start 5 sc in a magic ring [5]
Rnd 2 – 10: sc in all 5 st [5]
Change to off-white yarn.
Rnd 11: work this round in FLO, sc in next st, 3-dc-bobble in next 3 st, sc in next st [5]
Fasten off, leaving a long tail for sewing 8.
The arms don't need to be stuffed.

SKIRT

→ *start in light yellow yarn*

Leave a 4" / 10 cm long starting yarn tail, this will later be used to join Goldilocks and the bears together.
Rnd 1: start 6 sc in a magic ring [6]
Rnd 2: inc in all 6 st [12]
Rnd 3: (sc in next st, inc in next st) repeat 6 times [18]
Rnd 4: (sc in next st, inc in next st, sc in next st) repeat 6 times [24]
Rnd 5: (sc in next 3 st, inc in next st) repeat 6 times [30]
Rnd 6: (sc in next 2 st, inc in next st, sc in next 2 st) repeat 6 times [36]
Rnd 7: (sc in next 5 st, inc in next st) repeat 6 times [42]
Rnd 8: (sc in next 3 st, inc in next st, sc in next 3 st) repeat 6 times [48]
Rnd 9 – 10: sc in all 48 st [48]
Rnd 11: (sc in next 7 st, inc in next st) repeat 6 times [54]
Rnd 12 – 16: sc in all 54 st [54]
Rnd 17: (sc in next 4 st, inc in next st, sc in next 4 st) repeat 6 times [60]
Rnd 18: sc in all 60 st [60]
Change to off-white yarn. Don't fasten off the light yellow yarn, but bring the yarn to the outside.
Rnd 19: BLO sc in all 60 st [60]
Rnd 20 – 22: sc in all 60 st [60]
Change to yellow yarn. Don't fasten off the off-white yarn, but bring the yarn to the outside.

Rnd 23: BLO sc in all 60 st [60]
Rnd 24: (sc in next 9 st, inc in next st) repeat 6 times [66]
Rnd 25 – 27: sc in all 66 st [66]
Fasten off with an invisible join and weave in the yarn end.

Make frills in the front loops left on round 18. Hold the skirt with the open side facing you. Insert your hook in the first front loop and pull up a loop of the light yellow yarn 9.
Round of frills: work this round in FLO, (skip next st, 3 hdc in next st, skip next st, slst in next st) repeat 15 times, slst in first st [60] 10
Fasten off and weave in the yarn end.

Make frills in the front loops left on round 22. Hold the skirt with the open side facing you. Insert your hook in the first front loop and pull up a loop of the off-white yarn 11.
Round of frills: work this round in FLO, skip the stitch where you pulled up a loop, 3 hdc in next st, skip next st, slst in next st, (skip next st, 3 hdc in next st, skip next st, slst in next st) repeat 14 times, slst in first st [60]
Fasten off and weave in the yarn end 12.

SKIRT RIBBON

→ *in peach yarn*

Rnd 1: start in a magic ring: (ch 4, 2 tr in the magic ring, ch 4, slst in the magic ring) repeat 2 times, (ch 9, start in second ch from hook, hdc in next 6 ch, sc in next ch, slst in next ch, slst in the magic ring) repeat 2 times.
Tighten the magic ring. Fasten off, leaving a long tail for sewing 13.
Fold the ribbon down 13. Wrap the yarn tail around the center of the ribbon and the ribbon tails, and make a knot to keep it in shape 14.

ASSEMBLY

- Position and sew the hair base on the head. At the back, the distance between the hair base and the body should be 3 rounds.
- Position and sew hair strands 1 and 7 to the back, just below the hair base 15. Leave the remaining hair strands unsewn.
- Sew the pigtails to the hair base, between rounds 5-6.
- Sew the hair ribbons on top of the pigtails 16.
- Flatten the opening of the arms and sew them to the body, between rounds 20 and 21.

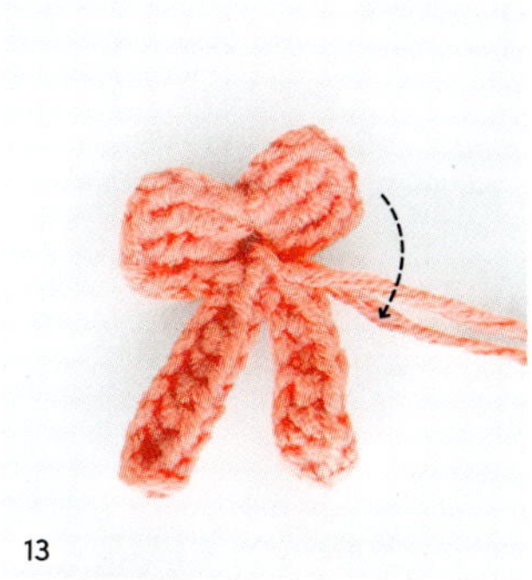

13

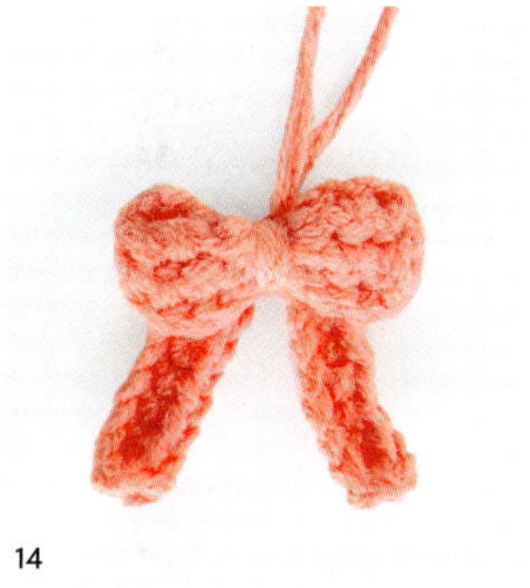

14

15

16

17

18

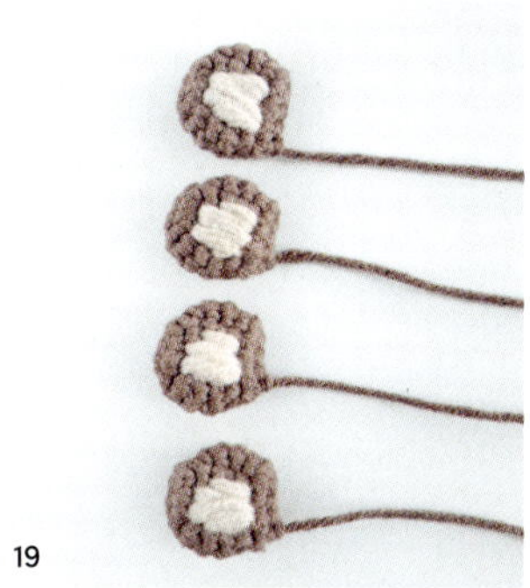

19

20

- Sew the body between rounds 4-5 of the skirt. Stuff the body with fiberfill before closing the seam.
- Sew the ribbon on one side of the skirt.

BEARS

BODY

→ *in dark brown yarn*

Leave a 4" / 10 cm long starting yarn tail, this will later be used to join Goldilocks and the bears together.
Rnd 1: start 6 sc in a magic ring [6]
Rnd 2: inc in all 6 st [12]
Rnd 3: (sc in next st, inc in next st) repeat 6 times [18]
Rnd 4: (sc in next st, inc in next st, sc in next st) repeat 6 times [24]
Rnd 5: (sc in next 3 st, inc in next st) repeat 6 times [30]
Rnd 6: (sc in next 2 st, inc in next st, sc in next 2 st) repeat 6 times [36]
Rnd 7: (sc in next 5 st, inc in next st) repeat 6 times [42]
Rnd 8: (sc in next 3 st, inc in next st, sc in next 3 st) repeat 6 times [48]
Rnd 9 – 10: sc in all 48 st [48]
Rnd 11: (sc in next 7 st, inc in next st) repeat 6 times [54]
Rnd 12 – 16: sc in all 54 st [54]
Rnd 17: (sc in next 4 st, inc in next st, sc in next 4 st) repeat 6 times [60]
Rnd 18 – 23: sc in all 60 st [60]
Rnd 24: (sc in next 9 st, inc in next st) repeat 6 times [66]
Rnd 25 – 27: sc in all 66 st [66]
Fasten off with an invisible join, leaving a 20" / 50 cm long yarn tail. This will later be used to sew Goldilocks and the bears together.

EAR

→ *make 2, start in cream yarn*

Start with a magic ring. Tighten but don't close the ring and continue crocheting in rows.
Row 1: start 6 hdc in a magic ring, ch 1, turn [6]
Change to dark brown yarn.
Row 2: inc in all 6 st [12]
Fasten off, leaving a long tail for sewing .

SNOUT

→ make 2, in cream yarn

Ch 4. Stitches are worked around both sides of the foundation chain.
Rnd 1: start in second ch from hook, sc in next 2 ch, 3 sc in next ch. Continue on the other side of the foundation chain, sc in next ch, inc in next ch [8]
Rnd 2: inc in next st, sc in next st, inc in next 3 st, sc in next st, inc in next 2 st [14]
Rnd 3: inc in next st, sc in next 3 st, inc in next st, sc in next 2 st, inc in next st, sc in next 3 st, inc in next st, sc in next 2 st [18]
Rnd 4 – 5: sc in all 18 st [18]
Fasten off, leaving a long tail for sewing.
Using black yarn, embroider a nose on each snout, over rounds 1-2.

PAW

→ make 4, in dark brown yarn

Ch 4. Stitches are worked around both sides of the foundation chain.
Rnd 1: start in second ch from hook, sc in next 2 ch, 3 sc in next ch. Continue on the other side of the foundation chain, sc in next ch, inc in next ch [8]
Rnd 2: (sc in next 3 st, 3 sc in next st) repeat 2 times [12]
Rnd 3 – 4: sc in all 12 st [12]
Rnd 5: (sc in next 4 st, dec) repeat 2 times [10]
The paws don't need to be stuffed.
Embroider a paw pad on each paw using cream yarn.
Flatten the opening of the paw and work the next round through both layers to close the opening. Skip 1 stitch on either end of the paw opening.
Rnd 6: sc in next 4 st [4] 18
Fasten off, leaving a long tail for sewing 19.

ARM

→ make 2, in dark brown yarn

Rnd 1: start 6 sc in a magic ring [6]
Rnd 2: inc in all 6 st [12]
Rnd 3: sc in all 12 st [12]

21 22

23

24

Rnd 4: (sc in next 4 st, dec) repeat 2 times [10]
Rnd 5 – 7: sc in all 10 st [10]
Note: *You can stuff the arm lightly with fiberfill, but stuffing is optional*
Flatten the opening of the arm and work the next round through both layers to close the opening. Skip 1 stitch on either end of the arm opening.
Rnd 8: sc in next 4 st [4]
Fasten off, leaving a long tail for sewing.

BABY BEAR

BODY

→ *in light brown yarn*

Rnd 1: start 6 sc in a magic ring [6]
Rnd 2: inc in all 6 st [12]
Rnd 3: (sc in next st, inc in next st) repeat 6 times [18]
Rnd 4: (sc in next 5 st, inc in next st) repeat 3 times [21]
Rnd 5 – 6: sc in all 21 st [21]
Rnd 7: sc in next 6 st, 3-dc-bobble in next st, sc in next 7 st, 3-dc-bobble in next st, sc in next 6 st [21]
Rnd 8 – 9: sc in all 21 st [21]
Rnd 10: sc in next 5 st, dec, 3-dc-bobble in next st, sc in next 3 st, 3-dc-bobble in next st, dec, sc in next 5 st, dec [18]
Rnd 11: (sc in next st, dec) repeat 6 times [12]
Stuff the body lightly with fiberfill.
Rnd 12: dec repeat 6 times [6]
Fasten off, leaving a long tail for sewing. Using your yarn needle, weave the yarn tail through the front loop of each remaining stitch and pull it tight to close.
Don't fasten off, but bring the yarn tail to the back of the body (use the bobble stitches for the legs as a reference point - these are slightly more at the front). We'll use this yarn tail for sewing later (20).

EAR

→ *make 2, in light brown yarn*

Pull up a loop of light brown yarn between rounds 2-3, on one side of the body, aligned with a bobble stitch of round 7 (21).
Row 1: ch 2, start in second ch from hook, sc in this ch [1]
Fasten off, leaving a yarn tail. Take the yarn tail on your needle and bring it into the body between rounds 1-2 (22). Weave in the yarn end. Repeat for the other side (23).

SNOUT

→ *in cream yarn*

Rnd 1: start 5 sc in a magic ring [5]
Slst in first st. Fasten off, leaving a long tail for sewing.

RIBBON

→ *make 1 in peach yarn, and 1 in black yarn*

Repeat the pattern for the hair ribbon on p. 95 (24).

ASSEMBLY

The bear has 2 sides: mommy bear and daddy bear. They share the same ears and arms, but have their own snout and paws (25).

- Sew the ears on top of the body, between rounds 5-9.
- Sew the snout between rounds 13-17, on each bear

25

26

27

28

side. Stuff the snout lightly with fiberfill before closing the seam.

- Sew the arms between rounds 18-19.
- Using black yarn, embroider the eyes on each bear side, 1 stitch from the snout.
  For mommy bear: embroider closed eyes on round 13, 3 stitches wide. Split your black yarn in strands and use a single strand to embroider the eyelashes.
  For daddy bear: embroider the eyes between rounds 12-13. Using black yarn, embroider the eyebrows on round 10. Using white yarn, embroider a flare on the eyes.
- Using peach yarn, embroider rosy cheeks for both bears, 2 stitches wide, between rounds 14-15.

- Sew the baby bear's snout to round 5 of its body. Using black yarn, embroider the eyes on round 4 and embroider the nose on the snout. Using peach yarn, embroider rosy cheeks between rounds 4-5.
- Sew the baby bear below the snout on the mommy bear side.
- Sew the paws on the last 5 rounds on both bear sides (on the mommy bear side: just beside baby bear).
- Sew the black ribbon below the snout of daddy bear.
- Sew the peach ribbon near the right ear of mommy bear.

JOINING GOLDILOCKS & THE BEARS

Flip Goldilocks and the bears inside out, so that the wrong sides of both are outward. Make a knot with the yarn tails left from the magic rings. Aim to leave a small space between both pieces 26.

Flip the bears back, so the right side is outward. Don't flip Goldilocks back, but keep her with the wrong side outward. The pieces don't need to be stuffed. Gently push Goldilocks inside the bears 27.

With the dark brown yarn tail left on the body of the bears, sew the last round of both the bears and Goldilocks together, using only the back loops on both rounds for sewing 28.

REVERSIBLE LILY FAIRY

SKILL LEVEL

★★★

SIZE

6" / 15 cm tall when made with the indicated yarn.

MATERIALS

- Sport weight yarn in:
  - pink
  - light pink
  - pale green
  - yellow
  - light peach
  - green
  - dark red
  - black (leftover)
- B-1 / 2.0 mm crochet hook
- Yarn needle
- Embroidery needle
- Stitch markers
- Fiberfill for stuffing
- Aluminum craft wire (0.5 mm, 6"/15 cm long)
- Optional: flower wire (gauge #22, 3.5"/ 9 cm long)
- Optional: pliers

Scan or visit www.amigurumi.com/5310 to share pictures and find inspiration.

PISTIL

start in light yellow yarn

Rnd 1: start 6 sc in a magic ring [6]
Change to pale green yarn. Don't fasten off the yellow yarn, but bring the yarn tail to the outside.
Rnd 2: BLO sc in all 6 st [6]
Rnd 3: sc in next st, dec, sc in next 3 st [5]
Rnd 4 – 7: sc in all 5 st [5]
Rnd 8: inc in all 5 st [10]
Rnd 9: (sc in next st, inc in next st) repeat 5 times [15]
Rnd 10: (sc in next 2 st, inc in next st) repeat 5 times [20]
Fasten off and weave in the yarn end.

Continue working with the light yellow yarn in the remaining front loops of round 1 (1).
Rnd 2: work this round in FLO, (ch 3, slst in next 2 st) repeat 2 times, ch 3, slst in next st [5]
Slst in the first front loop at the base of the initial ch-3.
Fasten off and weave in the yarn end (2).

INNER PETAL (3)

make 3, in pink yarn

Ch 15. Stitches are worked around both sides of the foundation chain before switching to rows.
Row 1: start in second ch from hook, hdc in next 9 ch, sc in next 4 ch, 3 sc in next ch. Continue on the other side of the foundation chain, sc in next 4 ch, hdc in next 9 ch, ch 1, turn [29]
Row 2: hdc in next 10 st, sc in next 4 st, 3 sc in next st, sc in next 4 st, hdc in next 10 st, ch 1, turn [31]
Row 3: hdc in next 7 st, sc in next 8 st, 3 sc in next st, sc in next 8 st, hdc in next 7 st, ch 1, turn [33]
Row 4: hdc in next 5 st, sc in next 2 st, inc in next st, sc in next 8 st, 3 sc in next st, sc in next 8 st, inc in next st, sc in next 2 st, hdc in next 5 st, ch 1, turn [37]
Row 5: sc in next 18 st, sc + ch-2-picot + sc in next st, sc in next 18 st, ch 1 [39]
Finishing row: don't turn, sc in next 10 row-ends along the straight side of the petal [10] (4)
On 2 petals, fasten off, leaving a 6" / 15 cm long yarn tail for sewing. On the third petal, don't fasten off.
Continue making the hair.

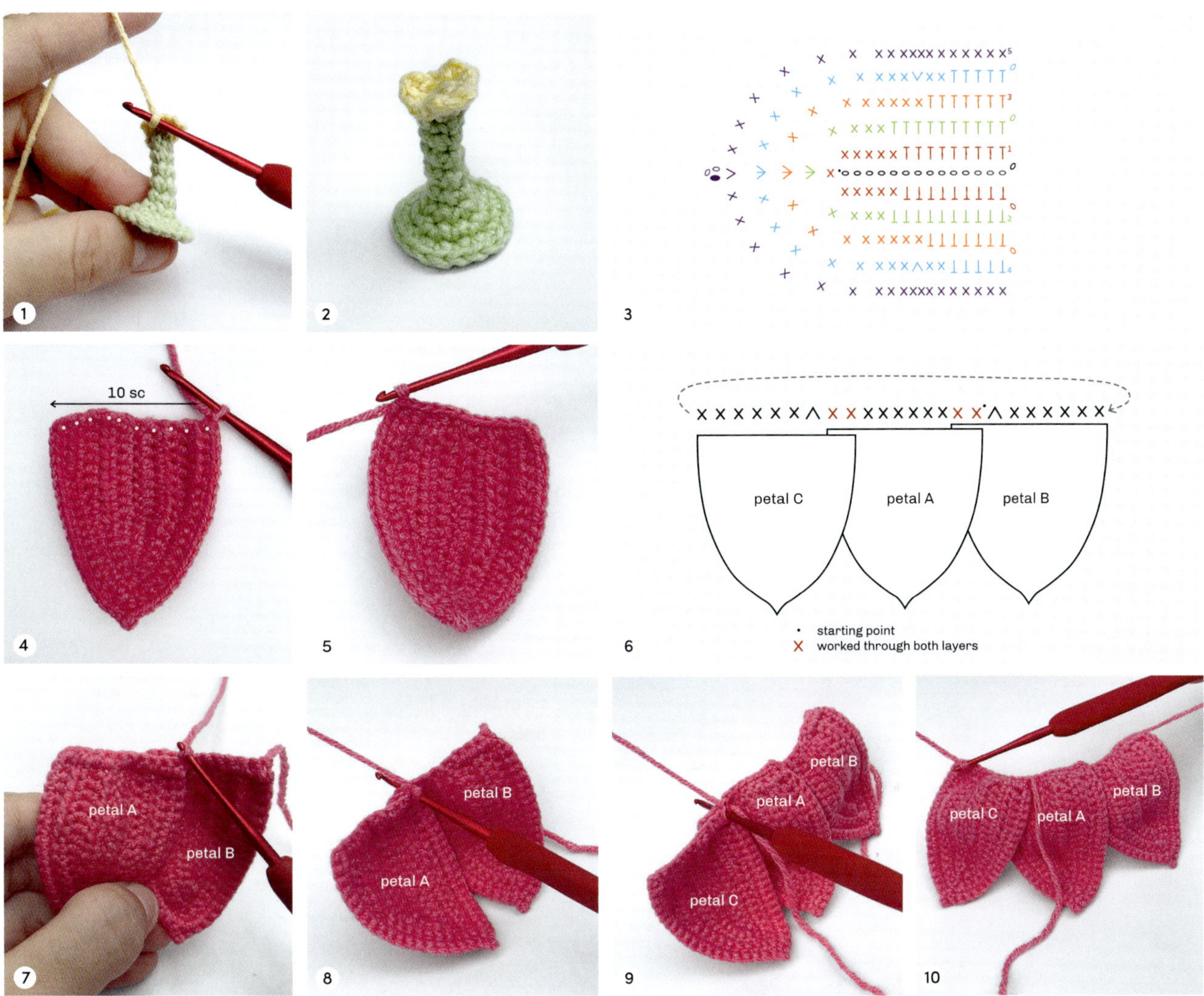

HAIR

→ *in pink yarn*

Make the hair by joining all 3 inner petals. Some parts of the petal overlap with the adjacent one. When petals overlap, you crochet through both layers at once 6. Turn your petals so that the wrong side is facing you. The last petal, with the active stitch, is petal A and the next petals are petal B and C. Take petal A, then put petal B to the right side, below petal A. The last 2 stitches of petal A should cover the first 2 stitches of petal B.

Continue crocheting with the pink yarn from petal A 7.

Rnd 1: ch 1, work through both petals: sc in next 2 st 8, work on petal A: sc in next 6 st.

Put petal C on top of petal A, so that the first 2 stitches of petal A are covered by the last 2 stitches of petal C. Work through both petals: sc in next 2 st 9, work on petal C: sc2tog, sc in next 6 st 10. Join to petal B to make a circle: sc in next 6 st, sc2tog [24] 11 12

Note: *The opening between petal C and B is for the face, which is why no stitches cover each other here.*

Rnd 2: (sc in next 4 st, dec) repeat 4 times [20] 13 14

Don't fasten off. Pause and sew the lower 3 stitches of petal A to petal B, and the lower 3 stitches of petal A to petal C. Use the remaining yarn tails from the petals, making sure not to sew more than 3 stitches at a time, so the petals can still open widely 15 16.

JOINING PISTIL AND HAIR

→ *in pink yarn*

Continue crocheting with the pink yarn. Position the pistil beneath the hair piece 17, making sure the last stitch of the hair aligns with the last stitch of the pistil 18.
Crochet the next round through both the stitches of the hair and the back loops of the pistil, leaving the front loops of the pistil free for creating the crown later.
Rnd 11: sc in all 20 st [20]
Rnd 12: (sc in next st, inc in next st, sc in next 2 st, inc in next st) repeat 4 times [28]

Rnd 13: (sc in next 2 st, inc in next st, sc in next 3 st, inc in next st) repeat 4 times [36] 19
Sc in next 8 st to reach the center back of the head.
Mark the next stitch as the new beginning of the next rounds.
Don't fasten off. Pause to make the crown.

CROWN AND STAMEN

→ *in pale green yarn*

The crown is crocheted into the remaining front loops of round 10. Prepare a thin wire to be inserted as you work the first round 20. Pull up a loop of pale green yarn in the third remaining front loop 21. Work the first stitch in the same stitch where you attached the yarn.
Rnd 1: ch 1, sc in next 2 st, then begin inserting the wire 22. The wire tail should be about 1 cm taller than the pistil, with the tip bent into an eyelet, (sc in next 6 st over the wire, make a loop with the wire about 1 cm taller than the pistil), repeat 2 times 23 24, sc in next 6 st over the wire [20]
Rnd 2: continue crocheting over the wire, slst in next st, skip 1 st, hdc inc in next st. Stop crocheting over the wire and cut the wire 1 cm taller than the pistil, bend the tip into an eyelet. Ch-2-picot + hdc inc in the same st as previous hdc inc, skip 1 st, slst in next 2 st, skip 2 st, dc inc + ch-2-picot + dc inc in next st, skip 2 st, slst in next 2 st, skip 1 st, hdc inc + ch-2-picot + hdc inc in next st, skip 1 st, slst in next st. Leave the remaining stitch unworked.
Fasten off and weave in the yarn ends 26.
Cut the wire at the top of each loop and bend each tip into an eyelet. You now have 6 stamens 27.

Wrap each stamen with yarn, starting with dark red yarn at the top and switching to pale green yarn for the stalk.
First, take the dark red yarn and tie a knot in the top loop. Wrap the yarn around the loop three times, then push it up to cover the top 28. Continue wrapping until the loop is fully covered in dark red yarn, then tie a knot to secure the end.
Next, use pale green yarn to wrap along the wire of the stalk. Once you reach the bottom, tie a knot 29 and weave in the yarn end. Repeat for all 6 stamens.

petal B
petal C
11
petal A
petal B
petal C
12
petal A
petal C
petal B
13
petal B
petal C
petal A
14
15
16
17
18
19
sk
sk
sk
sk
sk
sk
sk
sk
sk
= wire
20
21
22
23
24
25
26

HEAD

→ *continue in pink yarn*

Continue crocheting with the pink yarn. Work with 2 colors, alternating pink and light peach yarn. The color change is indicated in italics.

Note: *I use the cut-and-tie technique (p. 17). It's a bit time-consuming, but limits tension issues or colors popping through.*

Rnd 14: *(pink)* sc in next 15 st, *(light peach)* sc in next 6 st, *(pink)* sc in next 15 st [36]

Rnd 15: *(pink)* sc in next 14 st, *(light peach)* sc in next 8 st, *(pink)* sc in next 14 st [36]

Rnd 16: *(pink)* sc in next 13 st, *(light peach)* sc in next 10 st, *(pink)* sc in next 13 st [36]

Rnd 17 – 19: *(pink)* sc in next 13 st, *(light peach)* sc in next 11 st, *(pink)* sc in next 12 st [36]

Change to light peach yarn.

Rnd 20: sc in all 36 st [36]

Rnd 21: (sc in next 4 st, dec) repeat 6 times [30]

Rnd 22: (sc in next 3 st, dec) repeat 6 times [24]

Rnd 23: (sc in next 2 st, dec) repeat 6 times [18]

Rnd 24: (sc in next st, dec) repeat 6 times [12]

Stuff the head firmly with fiberfill.

Rnd 25: BLO dec 6 times [6]

Fasten off, leaving a yarn tail. Using your yarn needle, weave the yarn tail through the front loop of each remaining stitch and pull it tight to close. Weave in the yarn end 30.

OUTER PETAL 31

→ *make 3, in light pink yarn*

Ch 28. Stitches are worked around both sides of the foundation chain before switching to rows.

Row 1: start in second ch from hook, sc in next 4 ch, hdc in next 18 ch, sc in next 4 ch, 3 sc in next ch. Continue on the other side of the foundation chain, sc in next 4 ch, hdc in next 18 ch, sc in next 4 ch, ch 1, turn [55]

Row 2: sc in next 5 st, hdc in next 18 st, sc in next 4 st, 3 sc in next st, sc in next 4 st, hdc in next 18 st, sc in next 5 st, ch 1, turn [57]

Row 3: sc in next 6 st, hdc in next 14 st, sc in next 8 st, 3 sc in next st, sc in next 8 st, hdc in next 14 st, sc in next 6 st, ch 1, turn [59]

Row 4: sc in next 7 st, hdc in next 11 st, sc in next 2 st, inc in next st, sc in next 8 st, 3 sc in next st, sc in next 8 st, inc in next st, sc in next 2 st, hdc in next 11 st, sc in next 7 st, ch 1, turn [63]

Row 5: sc in next 8 st, hdc in next 5 st, sc in next 18 st, sc + ch-2-picot + sc in next st, sc in next 18 st, hdc in next 5 st, sc in next 8 st [65]

Finishing row: ch 1, sc in next 8 row-ends along the straight side of the petal [8] 32

On 2 petals, fasten off, leaving an 8" / 20 cm long tail for sewing. On the third petal, don't fasten off, but continue making the skirt 33.

SKIRT

→ *in light pink yarn*

Hold the outer petals with the right side facing you. Continue crocheting with the light pink yarn from the third petal.

Rnd 1: work this round by joining each petal one by one, start working on the second petal, continue on the first and end on the last petal: (sc in next 4 st, sc2tog) repeat

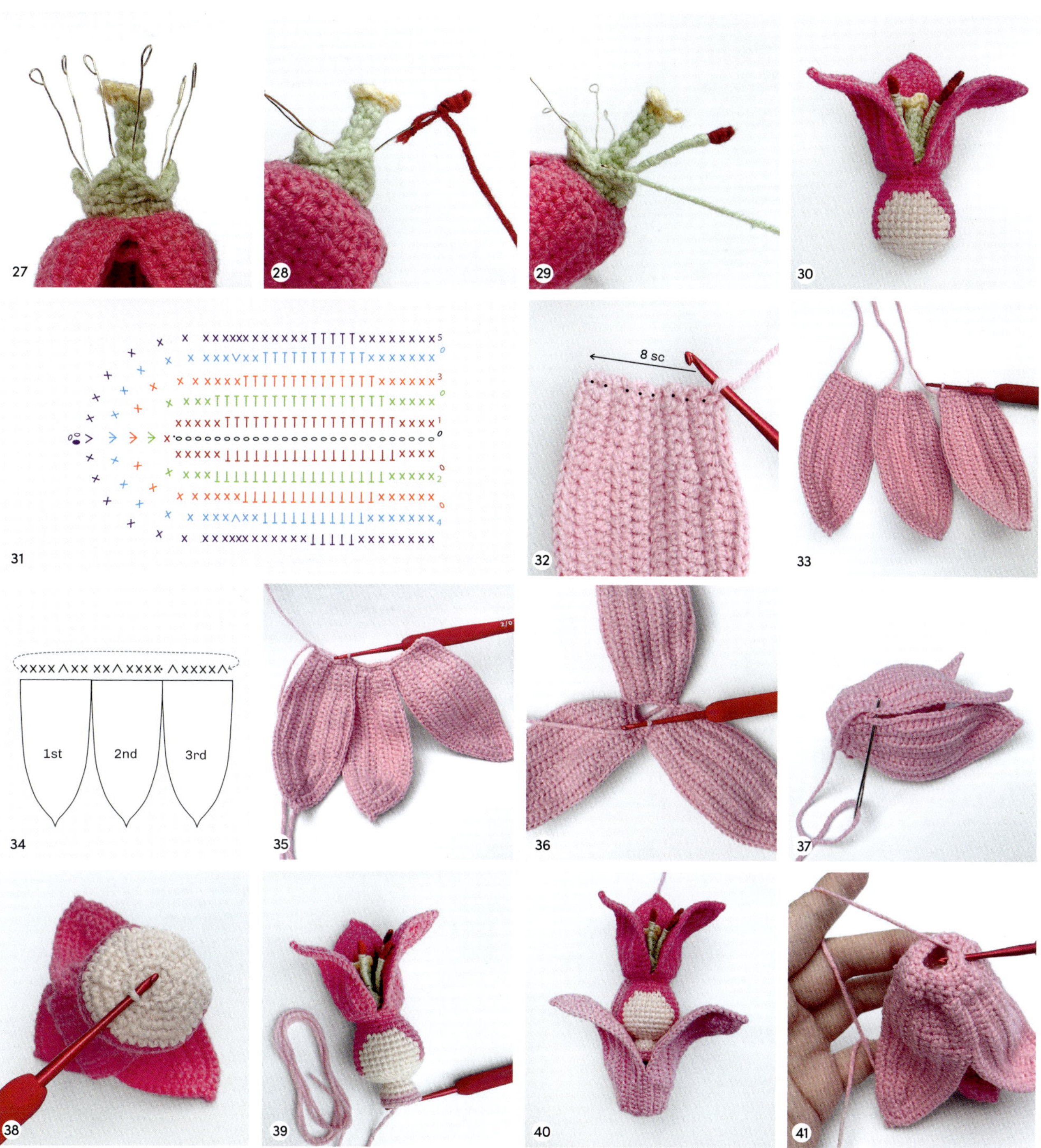

27 28 29 30 31 32 33 34 35 36 37 38 39 40 41

4 times [20] 34 35
Rnd 2: (sc in next 8 st, sc2tog) repeat 2 times [18] 36
Fasten off, leaving a long tail for sewing.
Sew the bottom 10 stitches of each pair of adjacent petals together, using the yarn tails of each petal 37.

BODY

→ *start in light peach yarn*

Hold the head upside down and pull up a loop of light peach yarn in the second front loop left on round 24 of the head 38. Work the first stitch in the same stitch where you attached the yarn.
Rnd 25: ch 1, FLO (sc in next st, inc in next st) repeat 6 times [18]
Rnd 26: sc in all 18 st [18]
Change to light pink yarn.
Rnd 27 – 28: sc in all 18 st [18]
Don't fasten off, but cut the light pink yarn, leaving a 20" / 50 cm yarn tail 39.
Flip the skirt so the petals' wrong sides face outward. Insert the body, aligning the last round of the body with the last round of the skirt 40.
Note: *The petals should be nested. If the position of yours looks different, fix it by twisting the body a little.*
Rnd 29: working through both layers of body and skirt, using the light pink yarn tail, sc in all 18 st [18] 41
Stuff the body with fiberfill.
Change to green yarn and continue making the stem.

STEM

→ *in green yarn*

Rnd 30: sc in all 18 st [18]
Stuff the stem with fiberfill and continue stuffing as you go.
Rnd 31: (sc in next 4 st, dec) repeat 3 times [15]
Rnd 32: (sc in next 3 st, dec) repeat 3 times [12]
Rnd 33: (sc in next 2 st, dec) repeat 3 times [9]
Rnd 34 – 42: sc in all 9 st [9]
Rnd 43: sc in next 3 st, dec, sc in next 4 st [8]
Rnd 44 – 45: sc in next 8 st [8]
Rnd 46: sc in next 3 st, dec, sc in next 3 st [7]
Rnd 47 – 48: sc in all 7 st [7]

Rnd 49: sc in next 2 st, dec, sc in next 3 st [6]
Rnd 50 – 52: sc in all 6 st [6]
Fasten off, leaving a yarn tail.
Optional: *To make the stem sturdier and bendable, you can insert wire into it. Take a piece of wire and bend one end into an eyelet. Cut the wire to the length of the stem + 1 cm. Wrap the bent end with yarn, then carefully insert the wire into the stem.*
Using your yarn needle, weave the yarn tail through the front loop of each remaining stitch and pull it tight to close. Weave in the yarn end (42).

LEAF

→ *in green yarn*

Ch 21. Stitches are worked around both sides of the foundation chain before switching to rows.
Row 1: start in second ch from hook, sc in next 4 ch, hdc in next 12 ch, sc in next 3 ch, 3 sc in next ch. Continue on the other side of the foundation chain, sc in next 3 ch, hdc in next 12 ch, sc in next 4 ch, ch 1, turn [41]
Row 2: sc in next 5 st, hdc in next 9 st, sc in next st, inc in next st, sc in next 4 st, sc + ch-2-picot + sc in next st, sc in next 4 st, inc in next st, sc in next st, hdc in next 9 st, sc in next 5 st [45]
Fasten off, leaving a long tail for sewing (43).

WING (44)

→ *make 2, in pale green yarn*

Ch 8. Crochet in rows.
Row 1: start in second ch from hook, slst in this ch, hdc in next ch, dc in next 3 ch, hdc in next ch, slst in next ch, ch 1, turn [7]
Row 2: skip 1 st, slst in next 2 st, ch 8, turn [2] Leave the remaining stitches unworked.
Row 3: start in second ch from hook, sc in next 2 ch, hdc in next 3 ch, sc in next 2 ch, slst in next st, ch 1, turn [8] Leave the remaining stitches unworked (45).
Row 4: skip 1 st, sc in next st, hdc in next 4 st, sc in next st, inc in next st, ch 1, turn [8]
Row 5: sc in next st, hdc in next st, hdc inc in next st, hdc in next 2 st, sc in next 2 st, slst in next st [9] (46)
Continue crocheting in the row-ends: inc in ch-space of row 4, slst in ch-space of row 2 (47) (48).
Fasten off, leaving a long tail for sewing (49).

ARM

→ *make 2, in light peach yarn*

Rnd 1: start 5 sc in a magic ring [5]
Rnd 2 – 11: sc in all 5 st [5]
Fasten off, leaving a long tail for sewing. The arms don't need to be stuffed.

ASSEMBLY

- Flatten the arms and sew them to the body over round 26.
- Sew the wings to the back, touching each other in the middle.
- Sew the leaf to the bottom 4 rounds of the stem.
- Embroider a halter top over rounds 26-27, using light pink yarn.
- Embroider the eyes over round 18, about 3 stitches wide, using black yarn.
- Split the black yarn in strands and use a single strand to embroider eyelashes over round 18.
- Split the pink yarn in strands and use a single strand to embroider a smile over round 20.
- Embroider rosy cheeks between rounds 19-20, 1 stitch wide, using pink yarn.

REVERSIBLE **LITTLE MERMAID**

SKILL LEVEL

★★★

SIZE

5.5" / 13.5 cm tall when made with the indicated yarn.

MATERIALS

- Sport weight yarn in:
  - light peach
  - purple
  - light purple
  - teal
  - light turquoise
  - coral
  - light gray
  - red
  - pink (leftover)
  - dark brown (leftover)
- B-1 / 2.25 mm crochet hook
- Safety eyes (7 mm)
- Googly eyes (5 mm)
- Yarn needle
- Embroidery needle
- Stitch markers
- Scissors
- Fiberfill for stuffing
- Fabric glue

Scan or visit www.amigurumi.com/5311 to share pictures and find inspiration.

Note: *For this type of reversible amigurumi, it's recommended to crochet the stitches a bit more loosely. I use a 2.25 mm crochet hook here instead of a 2 mm crochet hook. By sizing up my crochet hook, I can achieve a more relaxed tension, making it easier to flip the characters at the end.*

MERMAID

HEAD

→ *in light peach yarn*

Rnd 1: start 6 sc in a magic ring [6]
Rnd 2: inc in all 6 st [12]
Rnd 3: (sc in next st, inc in next st) repeat 6 times [18]
Rnd 4: (sc in next st, inc in next st, sc in next st) repeat 6 times [24]
Rnd 5: (sc in next 3 st, inc in next st) repeat 6 times [30]
Rnd 6 – 8: sc in all 30 st [30]
Rnd 9: (sc in next 9 st, inc in next st) repeat 3 times [33]
Rnd 10 – 14: sc in all 33 st [33]
Rnd 15: (sc in next 9 st, dec) repeat 3 times [30]
Rnd 16: (sc in next 3 st, dec) repeat 6 times [24]
Rnd 17: (sc in next 2 st, dec) repeat 6 times [18]
Rnd 18: (sc in next st, dec) repeat 6 times [12]
Stuff the head firmly with fiberfill.
Rnd 19: BLO dec 6 times [6]
Fasten off, leaving a yarn tail. Using your yarn needle, weave the yarn tail through the front loop of each remaining stitch and pull it tight to close. Weave in the yarn end.

- Using dark brown yarn, embroider the eyes, 2 stitches wide, on round 11. The distance between the eyes should be 5 stitches.
- Split your dark brown yarn in strands and use a single strand to embroider the eyelashes on round 11 and the eyebrows, 3 stitches wide, on round 8.
- Using coral yarn, embroider rosy cheeks between rounds 12-13.
- Split your pink yarn in strands and use a single strand to embroider a smile on round 13 ❶.

BODY

→ *start in light peach yarn*

Hold the head upside down and pull up a loop of light peach yarn in the second front loop left on round 18 ❷. Work the first stitch in the same stitch where you attached the yarn.
Rnd 19: ch 1, FLO (sc in next st, inc in next st) repeat 6 times [18]
Rnd 20: (sc in next 5 st, inc in next st) repeat 3 times [21]
Change to light purple yarn.

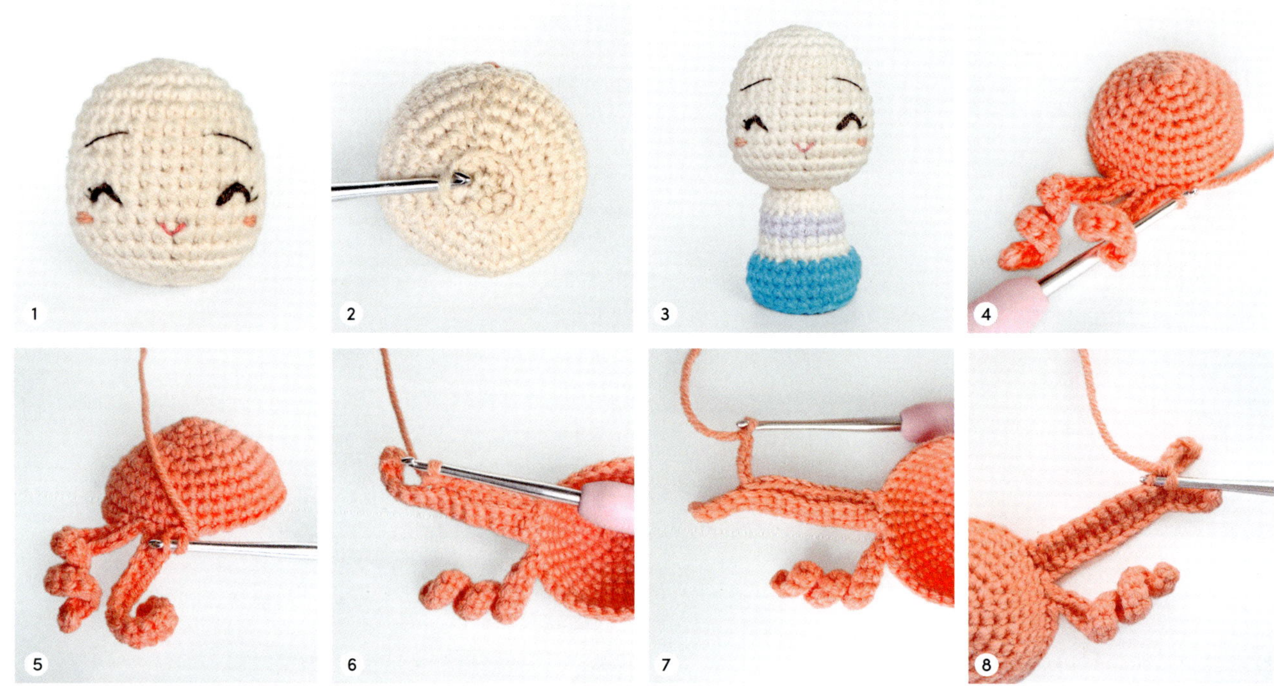

Rnd 21 – 22: sc in all 21 st [21]
Change to light peach yarn.
Rnd 23: sc in all 21 st [21]
Rnd 24: (sc in next 6 st, inc in next st) repeat 3 times [24]
Change to teal yarn.
Rnd 25: FLO (sc in next 2 st, inc in next st) repeat 8 times [32]
Rnd 26 – 27: sc in all 32 st [32]
Rnd 28: (sc in next 6 st, dec) repeat 4 times [28]
Fasten off, leaving a long tail for sewing ❸.

HAIR

→ make 2, in coral yarn (one for the mermaid, one for the girl)

Rnd 1: start 6 sc in a magic ring [6]
Rnd 2: inc in all 6 st [12]
Rnd 3: (sc in next st, inc in next st) repeat 6 times [18]
Rnd 4: (sc in next st, inc in next st, sc in next st) repeat 6 times [24]
Rnd 5: (sc in next 3 st, inc in next st) repeat 6 times [30]
Rnd 6: (sc in next 2 st, inc in next st, sc in next 2 st) repeat 6 times [36]
Rnd 7 – 9: sc in all 36 st [36]
Rnd 10: slst in next st. Continue making the hair strands,
Strand 1: ch 24, start in second ch from hook, sc in next 21 ch, slst in next 2 ch,
Continue working on the hair base, slst in next 2 st,
Strand 2: ch 17, start in second ch from hook, sc in next 14 ch, dec,
Continue working on the hair base, slst in next 2 st ❹, turn,
Strand 3: work in BLO of the previous hair strand ❺: sc in next 9 st ❻, slst in next 2 st, ch 5, turn ❼.
Leave the remaining stitches unworked.
Strand 4: start in second ch from hook, sc in next 4 ch ❽, then work in BLO of the previous hair strand: sc in next 9 st ❾, dec,
Continue working on the hair base ❿, slst in next 2 st, turn ⓫,
Strand 5: work in BLO of the previous hair strand: sc in next 14 st, ch 1, turn,
Strand 6: work in BLO of the previous hair strand:

9

10

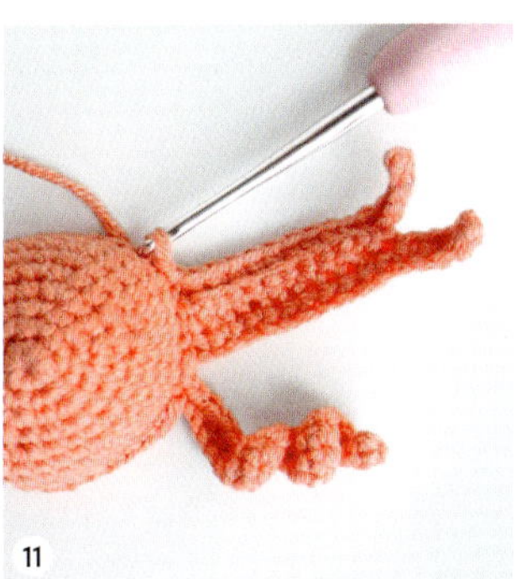
11

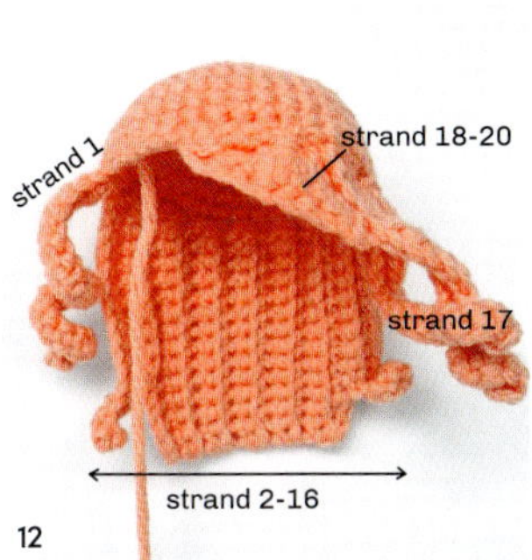

12

sc in next 12 st, dec,
Continue working on the hair base, slst in next 2 st, turn,
Strand 7: work in BLO of the previous hair strand:
sc in next 13 st, ch 1, turn,
Strand 8: work in BLO of the previous hair strand:
sc in next 13 st,
Continue working on the hair base, slst in next 2 st, turn,
Strand 9: work in BLO of the previous hair strand:
sc in next 13 st, ch 1, turn,
Strand 10: work in BLO of the previous hair strand:
sc in next 13 st,
Continue working on the hair base, slst in next 2 st, turn
Strand 11: work in BLO of the previous hair strand:
sc in next 13 st, ch 1, turn,
Strand 12: work in BLO of the previous hair strand:
sc in next 13 st,
Continue working on the hair base, slst in next 2 st, turn,
Strand 13: work in BLO of the previous hair strand:
sc in next 13 st, ch 1, turn,
Strand 14: work in BLO of the previous hair strand:
sc in next 12 st, inc in next st,
Continue working on the hair base, slst in next 2 st, turn,
Strand 15: work in BLO of the previous hair strand:
sc in next 8 st, slst in next 2 st, ch 5, turn. Leave the remaining stitches unworked.
Strand 16: start in second ch from hook, sc in next 4 ch, then work in BLO of the previous hair strand:
sc in next 9 st, inc in next st,
Continue working on the hair base, slst in next 2 st,
Strand 17: ch 24, start in second ch from hook,
sc in next 22 ch, inc in next ch,
Continue working on the hair base, skip 1 st, slst in next st,
Strand 18: ch 17, start in second ch from hook, sc in next 11 ch, hdc in next 3 ch, dc in next ch, 3 dc in next ch,
Continue working on the hair base, skip next 3 st, slst in next 2 st, turn,
Strand 19: work in BLO of the previous hair strand:
sc in next 3 st, slst in next 2 st, ch 1, turn. Leave the remaining stitch unworked.
Strand 20: work in BLO of the previous hair strand:
skip next st, sc in next st, hdc in next st, dc in next st,
3 dc + tr + dtr in next st,
Continue working on the hair base, skip next 4 st, slst in next 6 st.
Fasten off, leaving a long tail for sewing. Flip the hair base inside out, so that the wrong side is facing outward. Hide the starting yarn tail on the inside by passing it through the magic ring (12).

ARM

→ *make 2, in light peach yarn*

Rnd 1: start 5 sc in a magic ring [5]
Rnd 2 – 11: sc in all 5 st [5]
Fasten off, leaving a long tail for sewing. The arms don't need to be stuffed.

ROCK

→ *in light gray yarn*

Leave a 4" / 10 cm long starting yarn tail, this will later be used to join the little mermaid and the girl together.
Rnd 1: start 7 sc in a magic ring [7]
Rnd 2: inc in all 7 st [14]
Rnd 3: (sc in next st, inc in next st) repeat 7 times [21]
Rnd 4: (sc in next st, inc in next st, sc in next st) repeat

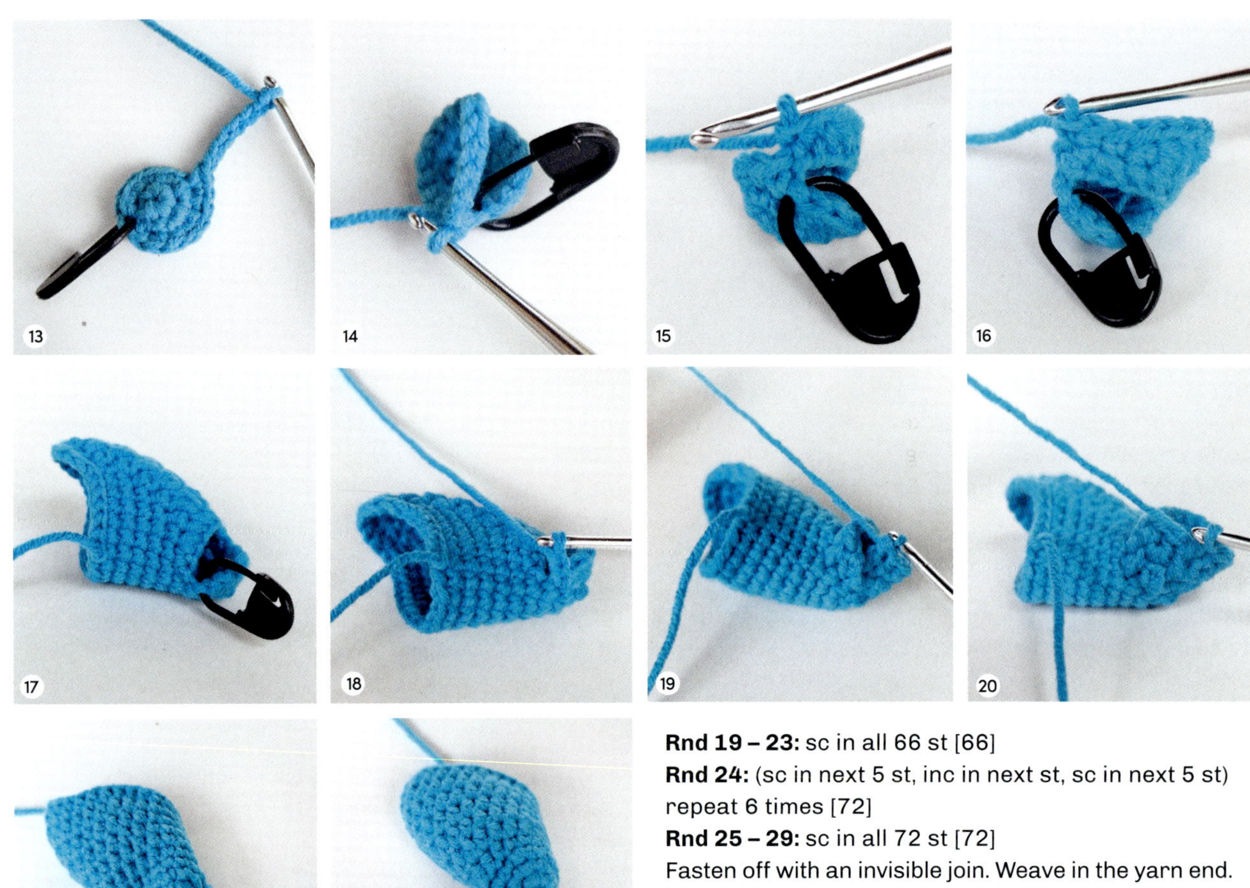

7 times [28]
Rnd 5: (sc in next 3 st, inc in next st) repeat 7 times [35]
Rnd 6: (sc in next 2 st, inc in next st, sc in next 2 st) repeat 7 times [42]
Rnd 7: (sc in next 5 st, inc in next st) repeat 7 times [49]
Rnd 8: sc in all 49 st [49]
Rnd 9: (sc in next 3 st, inc in next st, sc in next 3 st) repeat 7 times [56]
Rnd 10 – 12: sc in all 56 st [56]
Rnd 13: (sc in next 13 st, inc in next st) repeat 4 times [60]
Rnd 14 – 17: sc in all 60 st [60]
Rnd 18: (sc in next 9 st, inc in next st) repeat 6 times [66]
Rnd 19 – 23: sc in all 66 st [66]
Rnd 24: (sc in next 5 st, inc in next st, sc in next 5 st) repeat 6 times [72]
Rnd 25 – 29: sc in all 72 st [72]
Fasten off with an invisible join. Weave in the yarn end.

MERMAID TAIL

→ *in teal yarn*

Rnd 1: start 6 sc in a magic ring [6]
Rnd 2: inc in all 6 st [12]
Continue making the upper part of the tail.
Rnd 3a: (sc in next st, inc in next st) repeat 3 times, ch 7, skip next 6 st [9]
Count 7 stitches from the last stitch and mark this stitch with a stitch marker ⓭.
Rnd 4a: sc in marked stitch (don't remove the marker) ⓮, sc in next 5 st, hdc in next 3 st, hdc in next 5 ch, sc in next 2 ch [16] ⓯
Rnd 5a: sc in next 4 st, hdc in next 5 st, dc in next st, dc inc in next 2 st, hdc in next st, sc in next 3 st [18] ⓰
Rnd 6a: sc in next 4 st, hdc in next 6 st, dc in next st, dc inc in next 2 st, hdc in next st, sc in next 4 st [20]

Rnd 7a: sc in next 5 st, hdc in next 6 st, dc in next st, dc inc in next 2 st, hdc in next st, sc in next 5 st [22]
Rnd 8a: sc in next 5 st, hdc in next 7 st, dc in next st, dc inc in next 2 st, hdc in next st, sc in next 6 st [24]
Rnd 9a: sc in next 5 st, hdc in next 8 st, dc in next st, dc inc in next 2 st, hdc in next st, sc in next 7 st [26]
Rnd 10a: sc in next 5 st, hdc in next 9 st, dc in next st, dc inc in next st, dc in next st, hdc in next st, sc in next st, slst in next 7 st [27]
Fasten off, leaving a long tail for sewing 17.

Continue making the lower part of the tail. Pull up a new loop of teal yarn in the marked stitch on round 3.
Rnd 3b: ch 3 18, continue working in the other side of the ch, dc in next ch, hdc in next 6 ch, hdc inc in next st, sc in next 3 st, hdc in next st,
dc in next st [14] 19
Rnd 4b: dc in next st, hdc in next st, sc in next 5 st, inc in next st, sc in next 4 st, hdc in next 2 st [15] 20
Rnd 5b: dc in next st, sc in next 10 st, hdc in next 2 st, dc2tog [14] 21
Rnd 6b: hdc in next st, sc in next 4 st, inc in next st, sc in next 4 st, hdc in next 2 st, dc in next 2 st [15]
Rnd 7b: hdc in next st, sc in next 10 st, hdc in next 2 st, dc2tog [14]
Rnd 8b: hdc in next st, sc in next 4 st, dec, sc in next 4 st, hdc in next 3 st [13]
Rnd 9b: hdc in next st, sc in next 4 st, dec, sc in next 4 st, dec [11]
Rnd 10b: sc in next 5 st, dec, sc in next 4 st [10]
Rnd 11b: (dec, sc in next 3 st) repeat 2 times [8]
Fasten off, leaving a yarn tail. Using your yarn needle, weave the yarn tail through the front loop of each remaining stitch and pull it tight to close. Weave in the yarn end.
Stuff the mermaid tail lightly with fiberfill, but be careful not to overstuff 22.

CRAB 23

→ *in red yarn*

Rnd 1: start 6 sc in a magic ring [6]
Rnd 2: inc in all 6 st [12]
Rnd 3: (sc in next st, inc in next st) repeat 6 times [18]
In the next round, we make the legs and claws.

Rnd 4: Leg 1 and 2: (slst + ch-2-picot + slst in next st) repeat 2 times, slst in next 3 st,
Leg 3 and 4: (slst + ch-2-picot + slst in next st) repeat 2 times, slst in next 2 st,
Claw 1: ch 5, start in third ch from hook, hdc + sc in this ch, slst + ch-2-picot + slst in next ch, slst in next ch, slst in next 7 st,
Claw 2: ch 4, start in second ch from hook, slst in this ch, slst in next ch, ch 3, hdc + sc in third ch from hook, slst in the same ch where the previous slst was made, slst in next ch, slst in next 2 st.
Fasten off, leaving a long tail for sewing. The wrong side of the crab is the front side. Glue a pair of googly eyes at the top of the piece, between the claws 24.

MERMAID FIN 25

→ *make 2, in light turquoise yarn*

Ch 12. Crochet in rows.
Row 1: start in second ch from hook, slst in next 2 ch,

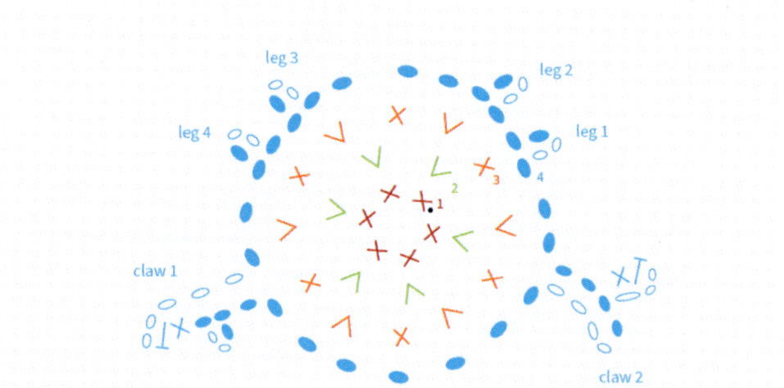

23

24

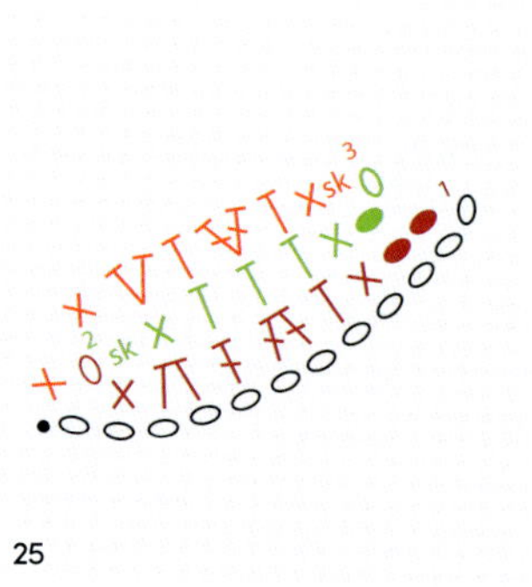

25

26

27

28

29

30

31

sc in next ch, hdc in next ch, dc2tog, dc in next ch, hdc2tog, sc in next ch, ch 1, turn [8] Leave the remaining chain unworked.

Row 2: skip first sc, sc in next st, hdc in next 3 st, sc in next st, slst in next st, ch 1, turn [6] Leave the remaining stitch unworked.

Row 3: skip first slst, sc in next st, hdc in next st, dc inc in next st, hdc in next st, hdc inc in next st [7] Sc in the chain gap of row 2, then sc in the last ch of the foundation chain.

Fasten off, leaving a long tail for sewing (26).

ASSEMBLY

- Position the hair on the head (27). Round 9 of the hair base is positioned diagonally on top of the head, and covers up to round 5 at the front of the head and approx. round 12 at the back of the head. Make sure that the hair is centered at the back. Sew the hair base on.
- Bring strand 17 to the center back of the hair base. Pin it so that the tip of the strand is left loose (28) and sew it on. Bring strand 1 to the center back as well, pin it so that the tip of the strand is left loose, sew it on and wrap the tips of the hair strands around each other (29).
- Sew strands 18-20 to the head, next to the left cheek.
- Flatten the opening of the arms and sew them to the body, between rounds 20-21.
- Sew the body to the top of the rock, between rounds 4-5. Stuff the body with fiberfill before closing the seam.
- Flatten the opening of the mermaid tail (30), then sew it to rounds 25-28 of the body (31). Sew the tail tip to the rock as well, but leave the rest of the tail unsewn.
- Sew the tail fins to the bottom of the tail. Sew them to

the rock with a few stitches as well.

- Sew the crab to the side of the rock, covering the bottom 8 rounds of the rock.
- Embroider some starfish on the rock using pink yarn.

GIRL

HEAD

→ in light peach yarn

Rnd 1: start 6 sc in a magic ring [6]
Rnd 2: inc in all 6 st [12]
Rnd 3: (sc in next st, inc in next st) repeat 6 times [18]
Rnd 4: (sc in next st, inc in next st, sc in next st) repeat 6 times [24]
Rnd 5: (sc in next 3 st, inc in next st) repeat 6 times [30]
Rnd 6 – 8: sc in all 30 st [30]
Rnd 9: (sc in next 9 st, inc in next st) repeat 3 times [33]
Rnd 10 – 14: sc in all 33 st [33]
Insert the safety eyes between rounds 11-12. The distance between the eyes should be 7 stitches. Make sure that the beginning of the round is situated at the center back.

Rnd 15: (sc in next 9 st, dec) repeat 3 times [30]
Rnd 16: (sc in next 3 st, dec) repeat 6 times [24]
Rnd 17: (sc in next 2 st, dec) repeat 6 times [18]
Rnd 18: (sc in next st, dec) repeat 6 times [12]
Stuff the head firmly with fiberfill.
Rnd 19: BLO dec 6 times [6]
Fasten off, leaving a yarn tail. Using your yarn needle, weave the yarn tail through the front loop of each remaining stitch and pull it tight to close. Weave in the yarn end.

- Split dark brown yarn in strands and use a single strand to embroider the eyebrows, 3 stitches wide, on round 9.
- Using coral yarn, embroider rosy cheeks between rounds 12-13.
- Split your pink yarn in strands and use a single strand to embroider a smile on round 13 (32).

BODY

→ start in light peach yarn

Hold the head upside down and pull up a loop of light peach yarn in the second front loop left on round 18. Work the first stitch in the same stitch where you attached the yarn.
Rnd 19: ch 1, FLO (sc in next st, inc in next st) repeat 6 times [18]
Rnd 20: (sc in next 5 st, inc in next st) repeat 3 times [21]
Change to light purple yarn.
Rnd 21 – 24: sc in all 21 st [21]
Change to purple yarn.
Rnd 25: (sc in next 6 st, inc in next st) repeat 3 times [24]
Rnd 26: BLO (sc in next 5 st, inc in next st) repeat 4 times [28]
Fasten off, leaving a long tail for sewing.

OUTER LAYER OF SKIRT

→ in light turquoise yarn

Work the outer layer of the skirt in the front loops left on round 25 of the body. The opening of the outer skirt layer should be at the center of the body. Mark 2 front loops at the front center of the body. The first of them is the starting point for the outer layer — the last will

be the ending point. Hold the head upward and pull up a loop of light turquoise yarn in the first front loop (32). Crochet in rows.

Row 1: ch 2, FLO (dc in next st, dc inc in next st, dc in next st) repeat 8 times, ch 2, turn [32]

Row 2: (dc in next 3 st, dc inc in next st) repeat 7 times, dc in next 4 st, turn [39]

Row 3: skip next 2 st, 3 hdc in next st, dc in next 2 st, tr in next 2 st, tr inc in next st, (dtr in next 2 st, dtr inc in next st) repeat 7 times, dtr in next 2 st, tr inc in next st, tr in next 2 st, dc in next 2 st, 3 hdc in next st, skip next st, slst in next st, turn [49]

Row 4: skip next 2 st, work this row in BLO, 3 hdc in next st, (dc in next 3 st, dc inc in next st) repeat 2 times, tr in next 4 st, tr inc in next st, (dtr in next 5 st, dtr inc in next st) repeat 2 times, dtr in next 5 st, tr inc in next st, tr in next 4 st, (dc inc in next st, dc in next 3 st) repeat 2 times, 3 hdc in next st, skip next st, slst in next st [58]

Fasten off, leaving a long tail for sewing (33).

ARM

→ *make 2, start in light peach yarn*

Rnd 1: start 5 sc in a magic ring [5]

Rnd 2 – 8: sc in all 5 st [5]

Change to light turquoise yarn.

Rnd 9: work this round in FLO, inc in next 4 st, sc in next st [9]

Rnd 10 – 11: sc in next st, hdc in next 6 st, sc in next 2 st [9]

Rnd 12: dec 4 times, slst in next st [5]

Fasten off, leaving a long tail for sewing. The arms don't need to be stuffed.

SKIRT

→ *in light purple yarn*

Leave a 4" / 10 cm long starting yarn tail, this will later be used to join the mermaid and the girl together.

Rnd 1: start 7 sc in a magic ring [7]

Rnd 2: inc in all 7 st [14]

Rnd 3: (sc in next st, inc in next st) repeat 7 times [21]

Rnd 4: (sc in next st, inc in next st, sc in next st) repeat

7 times [28]
Rnd 5: (sc in next 3 st, inc in next st) repeat 7 times [35]
Rnd 6: (sc in next 2 st, inc in next st, sc in next 2 st) repeat 7 times [42]
Rnd 7: (sc in next 5 st, inc in next st) repeat 7 times [49]
Rnd 8: sc in all 49 st [49]
Rnd 9: (sc in next 3 st, inc in next st, sc in next 3 st) repeat 7 times [56]
Rnd 10 – 12: sc in all 56 st [56]
Rnd 13: (sc in next 13 st, inc in next st) repeat 4 times [60]
Rnd 14 – 17: sc in all 60 st [60]
Rnd 18: (sc in next 9 st, inc in next st) repeat 6 times [66]
Rnd 19 – 23: sc in all 66 st [66]
Rnd 24: (sc in next 5 st, inc in next st, sc in next 5 st) repeat 6 times [72]
Rnd 25: BLO sc in all 72 st [72]
Rnd 26 – 29: sc in all 72 st [72]
Fasten off with an invisible join, leaving a 20" / 50 cm long yarn tail. This will later be used to sew the mermaid and the girl together.

Hold the skirt with the open side downward. Pull up a loop of white yarn in a front loop left on round 24 (34). Work the first stitch in the same stitch where you attached the yarn.
Frills round: FLO (slst in next st, skip 1 st, 4 hdc in next st, skip 1 st) repeat 18 times [90]
Slst in first st. Fasten off and weave in the yarn ends.

ASSEMBLY

- Repeat the instructions for sewing on the mermaid's hair on p. 112.
- Flatten the opening of the arms and sew them to the body, between rounds 20-21.
- Sew the body between rounds 4-5 of the skirt, using the purple yarn tail of the body. Stuff the body with fiberfill before closing the seam.
- Sew only the front edges of the outer layer to the skirt (35). Leave the rest of the outer layer unsewn.

JOINING THE MERMAID & GIRL

Flip the mermaid and the girl inside out, so that the wrong sides of both are outward. Make a knot with the yarn tails left from the magic rings. Try to leave a small space between both pieces (36).
Flip the girl back, so the right side is outward. Don't flip the mermaid back, but keep her with the wrong side outward. The pieces don't need to be stuffed. Gently push the mermaid inside the girl (37).
With the light purple yarn tail left on the skirt of the girl, sew the last round of both the girl and the mermaid together, using only the back loops on both rounds for sewing (38).

REVERSIBLE **RED RIDING HOOD & WOLF**

SKILL LEVEL

★★☆

SIZE

5" / 12 cm tall (doll side)
or 2.5" / 6.5 cm tall (wolf side)
when made with the indicated yarn.

MATERIALS

- Sport weight yarn in:
  - light peach
  - light brown
  - white
  - red
  - pink
  - dark brown
  - gray
  - peach (leftover)
  - black (leftover)
- B-1 / 2.25 mm crochet hook
- Safety eyes (6 mm)
- Yarn needle
- Embroidery needle
- Stitch markers
- Scissors
- Fiberfill for stuffing

Scan or visit
www.amigurumi.com/5312
to share pictures and find inspiration.

***Note:** For this type of reversible amigurumi, it's recommended to crochet the stitches a bit more loosely. I use a 2.25 mm crochet hook here instead of a 2 mm crochet hook. By sizing up my crochet hook, I can achieve a more relaxed tension, making it easier to flip the characters at the end.*

RED RIDING HOOD

HEAD

→ *in light peach yarn*

Rnd 1: start 6 sc in a magic ring [6]
Rnd 2: inc in all 6 st [12]
Rnd 3: (sc in next st, inc in next st) repeat 6 times [18]
Rnd 4: (sc in next st, inc in next st, sc in next st) repeat 6 times [24]
Rnd 5: (sc in next 3 st, inc in next st) repeat 2 times, continue working in BLO, (sc in next 3 st, inc in next st) repeat 2 times, continue working in both loops, (sc in next 3 st, inc in next st) repeat 2 times [30]
The 8 front loops left on round 4 will be used to make the hair bangs later.
Rnd 6 – 8: sc in all 30 st [30]
Rnd 9: (sc in next 9 st, inc in next st) repeat 3 times [33]
Rnd 10: (sc in next 5 st, inc in next st, sc in next 5 st) repeat 3 times [36]
Rnd 11 – 14: sc in all 36 st [36]
Insert the safety eyes between rounds 11-12, with the right eye aligned between the first and second front loops, as shown in 1. The distance between the eyes should be 7 stitches.
Rnd 15: (sc in next 4 st, dec) repeat 6 times [30]
Rnd 16: (sc in next 3 st, dec) repeat 6 times [24]
Rnd 17: (sc in next 2 st, dec) repeat 6 times [18]
Rnd 18: (sc in next st, dec) repeat 6 times [12]
Stuff the head firmly with fiberfill.
Rnd 19: BLO dec 6 times [6]
Fasten off, leaving a yarn tail. Using your yarn needle, weave the yarn tail through the front loop of each remaining stitch and pull it tight to close. Weave in the yarn end.

- Embroider rosy cheeks between rounds 12-13, using peach yarn.
- Split your pink yarn in strands and use a single strand to embroider a smile on round 13.

HAIR BANGS

→ *in light brown yarn*

With the girl's face facing you, pull up a loop of light brown yarn in the rightmost front loop on round 4 2.

Strand 1: ch 9, start in second ch from hook, slst in this ch, sc in next 7 ch,
Continue working on the head, skip the st where you attached the yarn, slst in next st,
Strand 2: ch 8, start in second ch from hook, slst in this ch, sc in next 6 ch,
Continue working on the head, skip next st, slst in next st,
Strand 3: ch 7, start in second ch from hook, slst in this ch, sc in next 5 ch,
Continue working on the head, skip next st, slst in next st,
Strand 4: ch 9, start in second ch from hook, slst in this ch, sc in next 7 ch,
Continue working on the head, skip next st, slst in next st.
Fasten off, leaving a long tail for sewing.
Bring strand 1 and 4 to each side, about 3-4 stitches from the safety eyes, and sew the tips of these strands to the head 3.

HAIR BRAID

→ make 2, in light brown yarn

Cut 12 strands of light brown yarn, about 6" / 15 cm long. Insert your crochet hook in the stitch next to the tip of the left hair bang, between rounds 11-12. Fold a light brown yarn strand in half, pull the loop through the stitch, then pull the ends through the loop and make a knot 4 5. Add 2 more strands next to the first one, so you have 3 strands attached in a row, between rounds 11-12. Attach 3 more strands just below them, between rounds 12-13 6.
Braid the yarn strands and tie the braid with another tail of light brown yarn 7. Cut off the excess yarn.
Repeat on the other side of the head.

BODY

→ start in white yarn

Hold the head upside down and pull up a loop of white yarn in the second front loop left on round 18 8. Work the first stitch in the same stitch where you attached the yarn.
Rnd 19: ch 1, FLO (sc in next st, inc in next st) repeat 6 times [18]
Rnd 20: (sc in next 5 st, inc in next st) repeat 3 times [21]

Change to dark brown yarn.
Rnd 21 – 22: sc in all 21 st [21]
Rnd 23: (sc in next 6 st, inc in next st) repeat 3 times [24]
Fasten off, leaving a long tail for sewing 9.

SKIRT

in pink yarn

Leave a 4" / 10 cm long starting yarn tail, this will later be used to join Red Riding Hood and the wolf together.
Rnd 1: start 6 sc in a magic ring [6]
Rnd 2: inc in all 6 st [12]
Rnd 3: (sc in next st, inc in next st) repeat 6 times [18]
Rnd 4: (sc in next st, inc in next st, sc in next st) repeat 6 times [24]
Rnd 5: (sc in next 3 st, inc in next st) repeat 6 times [30]
Rnd 6: (sc in next 2 st, inc in next st, sc in next 2 st) repeat 6 times [36]
Rnd 7: (sc in next 5 st, inc in next st) repeat 6 times [42]
Rnd 8: (sc in next 3 st, inc in next st, sc in next 3 st) repeat 6 times [48]
Rnd 9 – 10: sc in all 48 st [48]
Rnd 11: (sc in next 7 st, inc in next st) repeat 6 times [54]
Rnd 12 – 16: sc in all 54 st [54]
Rnd 17: (sc in next 4 st, inc in next st, sc in next 4 st) repeat 6 times [60]
Rnd 18 – 23: sc in all 60 st [60]
Rnd 24: (sc in next 9 st, inc in next st) repeat 6 times [66]
Rnd 25 – 27: sc in all 66 st [66]
Fasten off with an invisible join. Weave in the yarn end.

Hold the skirt upside down. Pull up a loop of white yarn between rounds 25-26.
Decorative round: surface slst in all 66 st [66] 10
Fasten off and weave in the yarn ends.

ARM

make 2, start in light peach yarn

Rnd 1: start 5 sc in a magic ring [5]
Rnd 2: sc in all 5 st [5]
Change to white yarn.
Rnd 3 – 11: sc in all 5 st [5]
Fasten off, leaving a long tail for sewing.
The arms don't need to be stuffed.

HOOD

in red yarn

Rnd 1: start 6 sc in a magic ring [6]
Rnd 2: (sc in next st, inc in next st) repeat 3 times [9]
Rnd 3: (sc in next 2 st, inc in next st) repeat 3 times [12]
Rnd 4: (sc in next 3 st, inc in next st) repeat 3 times [15]
Rnd 5: (sc in next 2 st, inc in next st) repeat 5 times [20]
Rnd 6: (sc in next 3 st, inc in next st) repeat 5 times [25]
Rnd 7: (sc in next 4 st, inc in next st) repeat 5 times [30]
Rnd 8: (hdc in next 4 st, hdc inc in next st) repeat 3 times, (sc in next 4 st, inc in next st) repeat 3 times [36]
Rnd 9: (hdc in next 5 st, hdc inc in next st) repeat 3 times, (sc in next 5 st, inc in next st) repeat 3 times [42]
Rnd 10: (hdc in next 3 st, hdc inc in next st, hdc in next 3 st) repeat 3 times, sc in next 21 st [45]
Rnd 11: hdc in next 4 st, hdc inc in next st, hdc in next

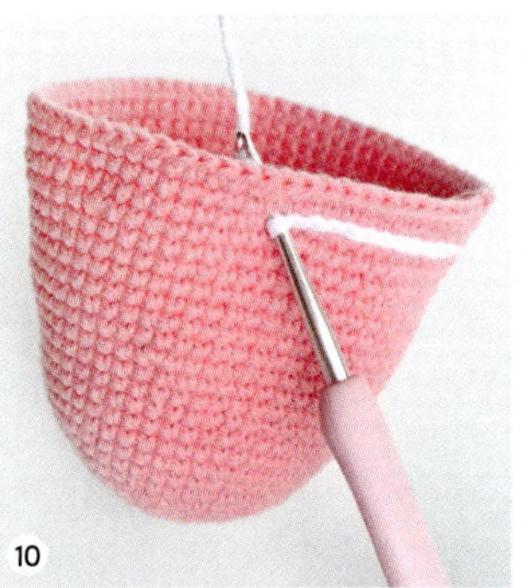

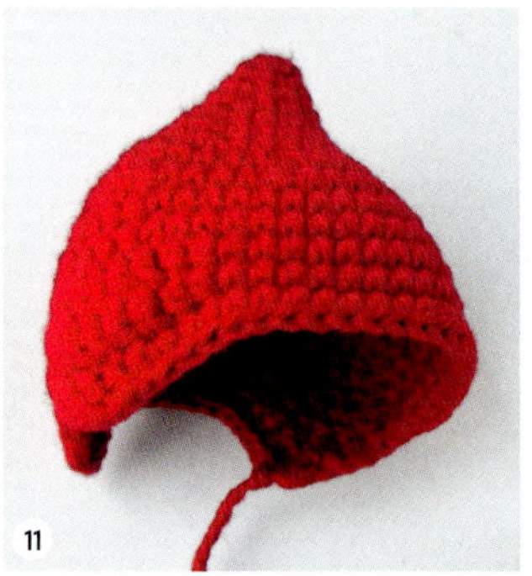

14 st, hdc inc in next st, hdc in next 4 st, sc in next 18 st, hdc in next 2 st, dc in next st [47]
Rnd 12: dc in next st, dc inc in next st, dc in next st, hdc in next 2 st, sc in next 16 st, hdc in next 2 st, dc in next st, dc inc in next st, dc in next 2 st, hdc in next 2 st, sc in next 15 st, hdc in next 2 st, dc in next st [49]
Rnd 13: dc in next 2 st, dc inc in next st, dc in next st, hdc in next 3 st, sc in next 14 st, hdc in next 3 st, dc in next st, dc inc in next st, dc in next 3 st, hdc in next 2 st, sc in next 18 st [51]
Rnd 14: hdc in next 2 st, dc in next st, dc inc in next 2 st, hdc in next 2 st, dec, (sc in next 5 st, dec) repeat 2 times, hdc in next 2 st, dc inc in next 2 st, dc in next st, hdc in next 2 st, sc in next 21 st [52]
Continue crocheting in rows.
Row 15: slst in next 5 st, ch 3, tr in next st, dc in next st, hdc in next st, (sc in next 3 st, dec) repeat 3 times, hdc in next st, dc in next st, tr in next st, ch 2, turn [23] Leave the remaining stitches unworked.
Row 16: dc in next st, hdc in next st, (sc in next 2 st, dec) repeat 3 times, sc in next 2 st, hdc in next st, dc in next st [15] Leave the remaining stitches unworked.
Fasten off, leaving a 6" / 15 cm long yarn tail for sewing 11.

With the last row facing you, pull up a loop of red yarn in the rightmost stitch (the first stitch of Row 16) 12. Leave a 6" / 15 cm long starting yarn tail for sewing. Crochet in rows. Start in the same stitch where you attached the yarn.
Row 1: ch 1, work this row in BLO, sc in first st, inc in next st, (hdc in next 2 st, hdc inc in next st) repeat 3 times, hdc in next 2 st, inc in next st, sc in next st, ch 1, turn [20]
Row 2: sc in next 3 st, hdc in next st, hdc inc in next st, (hdc in next 4 st, hdc inc in next st) repeat 2 times, hdc in next 2 st, sc in next 3 st, ch 1, turn [23]
Row 3: sc in next 2 st, inc in next st, (hdc in next 5 st, hdc inc in next st) repeat 2 times, hdc in next 5 st, inc in next st, sc in next 2 st, ch 1, turn [27]
Row 4: sc in next 4 st, hdc in next 2 st, hdc inc in next st, (hdc in next 6 st, hdc inc in next st) repeat 2 times, hdc in next 2 st, sc in next 4 st, ch 1, turn [30]
Row 5: sc in next 3 st, inc in next st, (hdc in next 7 st, hdc inc in next st) repeat 2 times, hdc in next 6 st, inc in next st, sc in next 3 st, ch 1, turn [34]
Row 6: sc in next 5 st, hdc in next 3 st, hdc inc in next st, (hdc in next 8 st, hdc inc in next st) repeat 2 times, hdc in next 2 st, sc in next 5 st, ch 1, turn [37]
Row 7: sc in next 4 st, inc in next st, (hdc in next 9 st, hdc inc in next st) repeat 2 times, hdc in next 7 st, inc in next st, sc in next 4 st [41]
Fasten off and weave in the yarn ends 13.

BASKET

→ in light brown yarn

Ch 6. Stitches are worked around both sides of the foundation chain.
Rnd 1: start in second ch from hook, sc in next 4 ch, 3 sc in next ch. Continue on the other side of the foundation chain, sc in next 3 ch, inc in next ch [12]
Rnd 2: inc in next st, sc in next 3 st, inc in next 3 st, sc in next 3 st, inc in next 2 st [18]
Rnd 3: sc in all 18 st [18]
Rnd 4: sc in next 17 st, ch 14, start in second ch from hook, slst in all 13 ch, slst in next st [31]

13

14

15

16

17

18

Fasten off, leaving a long tail for sewing.

Hold the basket upright. Pull up a loop of white yarn right next to the last stitch 14. Crochet in rows. Start in the same stitch where you attached the yarn.
Row 1: ch 1, sc in first st, hdc in next 5 st, slst in next st [7] Leave the remaining stitches unworked.
Fasten off and weave in the yarn ends 15.

APRON

→ in white yarn

Ch 5. Stitches are worked around both sides of the foundation chain before switching to rows.
Row 1: start in second ch from hook, sc in next 2 ch, hdc in next ch, 4 hdc in next ch. Continue on the other side of the foundation chain, hdc in next ch, sc in next 2 ch, ch 1, turn [10]
Row 2: sc in next 2 st, hdc in next st, hdc inc in next 4 st, hdc in next st, sc in next 2 st, ch 1, turn [14]
Row 3: skip next st, slst in next st, sc in next st, (hdc in next st, hdc inc in next st) repeat 4 times, sc in next st, slst in next 2 st [17]

Fasten off, leaving a long tail for sewing 16.

ASSEMBLY

- Using red yarn, embroider 3 "X" shapes on the dark brown part of the body as lacing 17.
- Flatten the opening of the arms and sew them to the body, between rounds 19 and 20.
- Sew the body to the skirt, between rounds 4-5. Stuff the body with fiberfill before closing the seam.
- Sew the apron at the front of the skirt, touching the dark brown part of the body 17.
- Sew the hood to the body, on the seam between the head and the body, using the leftover ending and beginning yarn tails.
- Sew the basket on one side of the skirt, starting 10 rounds below the dark brown part of the body. Then, sew the handle to the opposite side of the basket. Finally, sew one hand to the handle 18.

WOLF

BODY

→ in gray yarn

Leave a 4" / 10 cm long starting yarn tail, this will later be used to join Little Red Riding Hood and the wolf together.
Rnd 1: start 6 sc in a magic ring [6]
Rnd 2: inc in all 6 st [12]
Rnd 3: (sc in next st, inc in next st) repeat 6 times [18]
Rnd 4: (sc in next st, inc in next st, sc in next st) repeat 6 times [24]
Rnd 5: (sc in next 3 st, inc in next st) repeat 6 times [30]

19

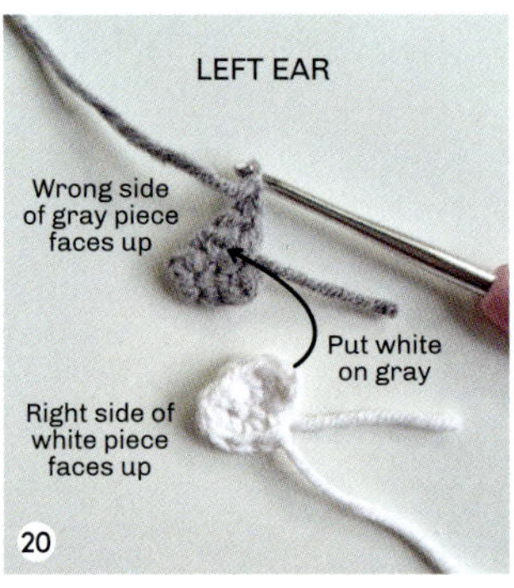

20

21

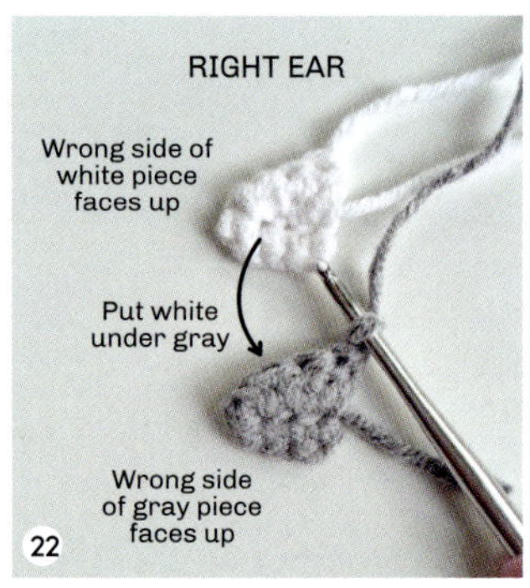

22

23

24

25

26

27

28

Rnd 6: (sc in next 2 st, inc in next st, sc in next 2 st) repeat 6 times [36]
Rnd 7: (sc in next 5 st, inc in next st) repeat 6 times [42]
Rnd 8: (sc in next 3 st, inc in next st, sc in next 3 st) repeat 6 times [48]
Rnd 9 – 10: sc in all 48 st [48]
Rnd 11: (sc in next 7 st, inc in next st) repeat 6 times [54]
Rnd 12 – 16: sc in all 54 st [54]
Rnd 17: (sc in next 4 st, inc in next st, sc in next 4 st) repeat 6 times [60]
Rnd 18 – 23: sc in all 60 st [60]
Rnd 24: (sc in next 9 st, inc in next st) repeat 6 times [66]
Rnd 25 – 27: sc in all 66 st [66]
Fasten off with an invisible join, leaving a 20" / 50 cm long yarn tail. This will later be used to sew Little Red Riding Hood and the wolf together.

EARS

The terms 'right' and 'left' mentioned in this pattern are based on the wolf's viewpoint. The left and right ear are worked differently.

LEFT EAR White piece

→ *in white yarn*

Ch 5. Stitches are worked around both sides of the foundation chain.

Rnd 1: start in third ch from hook, dc inc in this ch, hdc in next ch, 3 sc in next ch. Continue on the other side of the foundation chain, sc in next 2 ch [8]

Fasten off, leaving a short yarn tail (19).

LEFT EAR Gray piece

→ *in gray yarn*

Ch 4. Stitches are worked around both sides of the foundation chain before switching to rows.

Row 1: start in second ch from hook, sc in next 2 ch, 3 sc in next ch. Continue on the other side of the foundation chain, hdc in next ch, dc inc in next ch, ch 1, turn [8]

Pause to position the pieces. With the gray piece's wrong side facing up, put the white piece on top of the gray piece with the white piece's right side facing up (20).

In the next row, we'll join both pieces together, crocheting through the back loops of the white piece *(the loops closest to the gray piece)* and both loops of the gray piece (21). Since both pieces are mirrored, you work in the matching stitches.

Row 2: 3 hdc in next st, sc in next 3 st, sc + ch 2 + sc in second ch + sc in same st, sc in next 2 st, inc in next st [13]

Fasten off, leaving a long tail for sewing.

RIGHT EAR White piece

→ *in white yarn*

Ch 4. Stitches are worked around both sides of the foundation chain.

Rnd 1: start in second ch from hook, sc in next 2 ch, 3 sc in next ch. Continue on the other side of the foundation chain, hdc in next ch, dc inc in next ch [8]

Fasten off, leaving a short yarn tail.

RIGHT EAR Gray piece

→ *in gray yarn*

Ch 4. Stitches are worked around both sides of the foundation chain before switching to rows.

Row 1: start in second ch from hook, sc in next 2 ch, 3 sc in next ch. Continue on the other side of the foundation chain, hdc in next ch, dc inc in next ch, ch 1, turn [8]

Pause to position the pieces. Take the white piece and position it with the wrong side facing up. Put the gray piece on top of the white piece, with the gray piece's wrong side facing up (22).

In the next row, we'll join both pieces together, crocheting through the front loops of the white piece *(the loops closest to the gray piece)* and both loops of the gray piece (23). Since both pieces are mirrored, you work in the matching stitches.

Row 2: 3 hdc in next st, sc in next 3 st, sc + ch 2 + sc in second ch + sc in same st, sc in next 2 st, inc in next st [13]

Fasten off, leaving a long tail for sewing (24).

WHITE FUR (25)

→ *in white yarn*

Ch 22. Stitches are worked around both sides of the foundation chain.

Rnd 1: start in second ch from hook, slst in this ch, sc in next 3 ch, hdc in next 3 ch, dc in next 7 ch, hdc in next 3 ch, sc in next 3 ch, slst + ch-2-picot + slst + ch-2-picot + slst + ch-2-picot in next ch. Continue on the other side of the foundation chain, slst in next 20 ch, ch-2-picot + slst + ch-2-picot + slst + ch-2-picot + slst in next ch [52]

Rnd 2: skip 1 st, slst in next 3 st, sc in next st, (sc + ch 2 + sc in next st, slst in next st) repeat 2 times, skip 1 st, hdc inc + ch 2 + hdc inc in next st, skip 1 st, (slst in next st, sc + ch 2 + sc in next st) repeat 2 times, sc in next st, slst in next 3 st [24] Leave the remaining stitches unworked.

Fasten off, leaving a long tail for sewing (26).

SNOUT

→ *in white yarn*

Ch 4. Stitches are worked around both sides of the foundation chain.

Rnd 1: start in second ch from hook, sc in next 2 ch, 3 sc in next ch. Continue on the other side of the foundation chain, sc in next ch, inc in next ch [8]

Crochet 4 rounds using the jacquard technique (p.18), alternating gray and white yarn. The color changes are

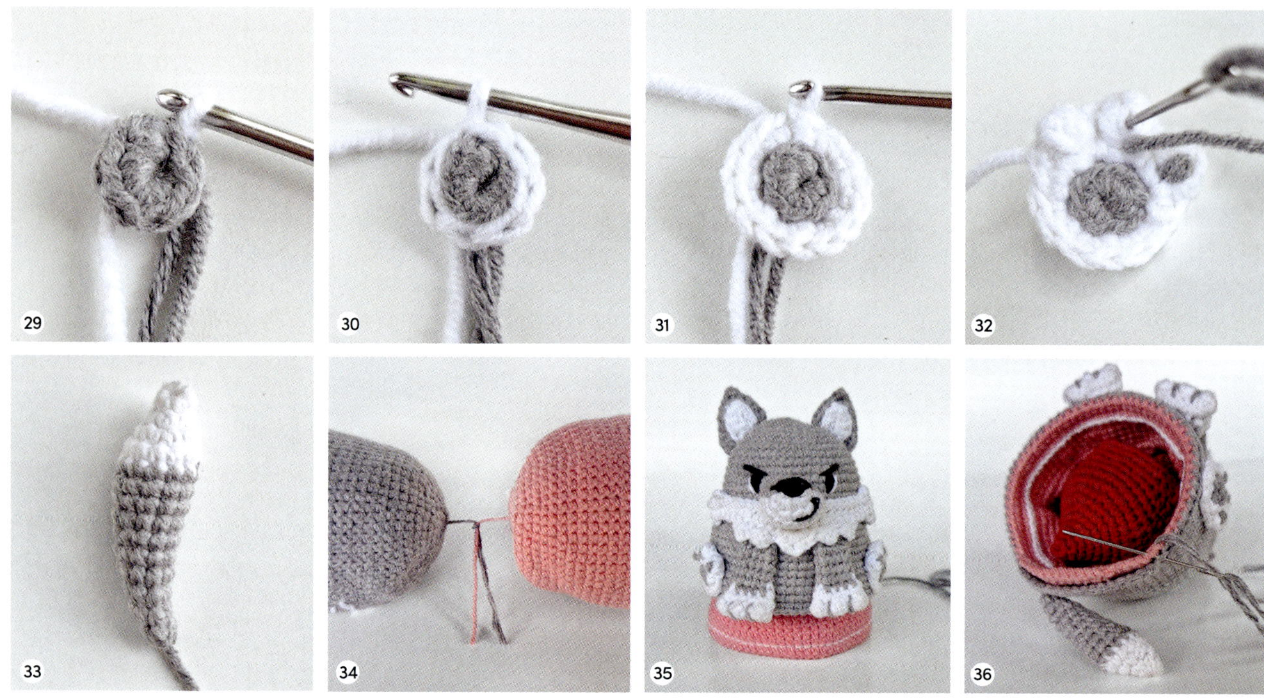

indicated in italics.
Rnd 2: *(gray)* inc in next st, sc in next st, inc in next st, *(white)* inc in next 2 st, sc in next st, inc in next 2 st [14]
Rnd 3: *(gray)* inc in next st, sc in next 3 st, inc in next st, *(white)* sc in next st, inc in next st, sc in next 5 st, inc in next st, sc in next st [18]
Rnd 4: *(gray)* sc in next 7 st, *(white)* sc in next 11 st [18]
Rnd 5: *(gray)* sc in next 7 st, *(white)* sc in next 10 st, slst in next st [18]
Fasten off, leaving long gray and white yarn tails for sewing.

- Using black yarn, embroider the nose over the gray side of rounds 1-2.
- Split your black yarn in strands and use a single strand to embroider the smile and fangs on round 2 (27).

FRONT LEG

→ *make 2, start in white yarn*

Ch 6. Stitches are worked around both sides of the foundation chain.
Rnd 1: start in second ch from hook, sc in next 4 ch, 3 sc in next ch. Continue on the other side of the foundation chain, sc in next 3 ch, inc in next ch [12]
Rnd 2: (3-dc-bobble in next st, slst in next st) repeat 2 times, 3-dc-bobble in next st, sc in next 7 st [12]
Rnd 3: sc in all 12 st [12]
Change to gray yarn.
Rnd 4: (sc in next 4 st, dec) repeat 2 times [10]
Rnd 5 – 8: sc in all 10 st [10]
The front leg doesn't need to be stuffed. Flatten the opening of the leg and work the next round through both layers to close the opening. Skip 1 stitch on either end of the leg opening.
Rnd 9: sc in next 4 st [4]
Fasten off, leaving a long tail for sewing. Using gray yarn, embroider a line between each bobble stitch (28).

PAW

→ *make 2, start in gray yarn*

Crochet in joined rounds.
Rnd 1: start 7 sc in a magic ring, slst in first st [7]

Change to white yarn. Fasten off the gray yarn, leaving a 6" / 15 cm long yarn tail for embroidery. The next stitch is the new beginning of the round 29.
Tip: *Work the slst in the next round rather loosely, so it's not too hard to work into them in Rnd 3.*
Rnd 2: BLO slst in next 7 st, slst in first st [7] 30
Rnd 3: ch 1, inc in next 7 st, slst in first st [14] 31
Rnd 4: skip the stitch where the last slst was made, (3-dc-bobble in next st, slst in next st) repeat 3 times [6]
Leave the remaining stitches unworked.
Fasten off with an invisible join, leaving a long tail for sewing. Embroider a paw pad on each bobble stitch using gray yarn 32.

TAIL

→ *start in white yarn*

Rnd 1: start 6 sc in a magic ring [6]
Rnd 2: sc in next 3 st, inc in next 3 st [9]
Rnd 3: sc in next 4 st, inc in next 3 st, sc in next 2 st [12]
Rnd 4: sc in next 7 st, inc in next st, sc in next 4 st [13]
Change to gray yarn.
Rnd 5 – 6: sc in all 13 st [13]
Rnd 7: sc in next st, dec, sc in next 10 st [12]
Rnd 8: sc in all 12 st [12]
Rnd 9: sc in next st, dec, sc in next 9 st [11]
Rnd 10: sc in all 11 st [11]
Rnd 11: sc in next st, dec, sc in next 8 st [10]
Rnd 12: sc in all 10 st [10]
Stuff the tail lightly with fiberfill.
Rnd 13: dec 2 times, sc in next 6 st [8]
Rnd 14: dec 2 times, sc in next 4 st [6]
Fasten off with an invisible join, leaving a long tail for sewing 33.

ASSEMBLY

- Sew the ears on top of the body, between rounds 4-9.
- Sew the white fur to the body, with its wrong side facing outward. Sew the flat side just below round 14 of the body. Don't sew the pointy parts down, they should cover the top of the front legs.
- Sew the snout to the body, with the white part on the white fur and the gray part on the body.
- Using black and white yarn, embroider the eyes between rounds 12-13, at 1 stitch from the snout.
- Using black yarn, embroider the eyebrows on round 11.
- Sew the front legs to the body, about 3-4 stitches apart, just below and centered to the white fur.
- Sew the paws at 3 stitches from the front legs.
- Sew the tail to the back, at 3 rounds above the last round.

JOINING RED RIDING HOOD & WOLF

Flip Red Riding Hood and the wolf inside out, so that the wrong sides of both are outward. Make a knot with the yarn tails left from the magic rings. Try to leave a small space between both pieces 34.
Flip the wolf back, so the right side is outward. Don't flip Red Riding Hood back, but keep her with the wrong side outward. The pieces don't need to be stuffed. Gently push Red Riding Hood inside the wolf 35.
With the gray yarn tail left on the body of the wolf, sew the last rounds of both the wolf and Red Riding Hood together, using only the back loops on both rounds for sewing 36.

REVERSIBLE TULIP FAIRY

SKILL LEVEL

★★☆

SIZE

4" / 10 cm tall when made with the indicated yarn.

MATERIALS

- Sport weight yarn in:
  - pink
  - peach
  - green
  - light peach
  - pale blue
  - light pink (leftover)
  - black (leftover)
- B-1 / 2.0 mm crochet hook
- Yarn needle
- Embroidery needle
- Stitch marker
- Fiberfill for stuffing
- Optional: flower wire (gauge #22, 3"/8 cm long)
- Optional: pliers

Scan or visit www.amigurumi.com/5313 to share pictures and find inspiration.

PETALS 1

→ *3 petals in peach yarn, 3 petals in pink yarn*

***Note:** Avoid crocheting the petals too tightly. If needed, use a larger hook to achieve a loose tension.*

Ch 13. Stitches are worked around both sides of the foundation chain before switching to rows.

Row 1: start in second ch from hook, hdc in next 4 ch, dc in next 5 ch, hdc in next 2 ch, 3 sc in next ch. Continue on the other side of the foundation chain, hdc in next 2 ch, dc in next 5 ch, hdc in next 4 ch, ch 1, turn [25]

Row 2: hdc in next 4 st, hdc inc in next st, hdc in next 6 st, inc in next 3 st, hdc in next 6 st, hdc inc in next st, hdc in next 4 st, ch 1, turn [30]

Row 3: hdc in next 8 st, hdc inc in next st, hdc in next 3 st, (sc in next st, inc in next st) repeat 3 times, hdc in next 3 st, hdc inc in next st, hdc in next 8 st, ch 1, turn [35]

Row 4: sc in next 14 st, (inc in next st, sc in next 2 st) repeat 3 times, sc in next 12 st, ch 1, turn [38]

Row 5: sc in next 17 st, 3 hdc in next st, slst in next 2 st, 3 hdc in next st, sc in next 17 st [42]

Fasten off, leaving a 4"/ 10 cm long yarn tail. Organize the petals by color and line them up. Sew 4 stitches of each petal together, then connect the last petal to the first to form a circle 2 3 4 5.

Pull up a loop of the same color yarn in a row-end on the flat side of a petal 6. Work the first stitch in the same stitch where you attached the yarn.

Rnd 1: ch 1, (sc in next 12 row-ends on the flat side) repeat for 3 petals [36] 7

***Note:** For rounds 2-4, use regular decreases instead of invisible decreases. An invisible decrease is worked in the front loops only. As both sides of the final work will be visible, I prefer using a regular decrease (sc2tog), worked through both loops.*

Rnd 2: (sc in next 4 st, sc2tog) repeat 6 times [30]

Rnd 3: (sc in next 3 st, sc2tog) repeat 6 times [24]

For the pink petals, fasten off with an invisible join. Count 4 stitches from the last stitches (5 stitches from the stitch made for the invisible join) and mark this stitch with a stitch marker 8.

Don't fasten off on the peach petals, we will continue to join both petal parts 9.

1
2
3
4
5
6
7
8
9
10
11
12
13
14
15

Flip the pink petal piece so the wrong side faces outward. Insert the pink petals into the peach petals, aligning the last round of the pink petals with the last round of the peach petals. In order to get nested petals, make sure to align the marked stitch on the pink petals piece with the last stitch of the peach petals piece 10. Continue working through both pink and peach petals at once.
Rnd 4: (sc in next 2 st, sc2tog) repeat 6 times [18]
Fasten off with an invisible join and weave in the yarn end. Count 3 stitches from the last stitch (4 stitches from the stitch made for the invisible join) and mark this stitch with a stitch marker 11.
The skirt will later be joined together with the body.

HEAD

start in pink yarn

Rnd 1: start 5 sc in a magic ring [5]
Rnd 2: inc in all 5 st [10]
Rnd 3: sc in all 10 st [10]
Rnd 4: (sc in next st, inc in next st) repeat 5 times [15]
Rnd 5: sc in all 15 st [15]
Rnd 6: (sc in next 2 st, inc in next st) repeat 5 times [20]
Rnd 7: (sc in next st, inc in next st, sc in next 2 st, inc in next st) repeat 4 times [28]
Rnd 8: (sc in next 2 st, inc in next st, sc in next 3 st, inc in next st) repeat 4 times [36]
Continue working with 2 colors, alternating pink and light peach yarn. The color change is indicated in italics.
***Note:** I use the cut-and-tie technique (p. 17). It's a bit time-consuming, but limits tension issues or colors popping through.*
Rnd 9: *(pink)* sc in next 15 st, *(light peach)* sc in next 6 st, *(pink)* sc in next 15 st [36]
Rnd 10: *(pink)* sc in next 14 st, *(light peach)* sc in next 8 st, *(pink)* sc in next 14 st [36]
Rnd 11: *(pink)* sc in next 13 st, *(light peach)* sc in next 10 st, *(pink)* sc in next 13 st [36]
Rnd 12 – 15: *(pink)* sc in next 13 st, *(light peach)* sc in next 11 st, *(pink)* sc in next 12 st [36]
Rnd 16: *(pink)* (sc in next 4 st, dec) repeat 2 times, sc in next 2 st, *(light peach)* sc in next 2 st, dec, sc in next 4 st, dec, *(pink)* (sc in next 4 st, dec) repeat 2 times [30]
Rnd 17: *(pink)* (sc in next 3 st, dec) repeat 2 times, sc in next 2 st, *(light peach)* sc in next st, dec, sc in next 3 st, dec, *(pink)* (sc in next 3 st, dec) repeat 2 times [24]
Rnd 18: *(pink)* (sc in next 2 st, dec) repeat 2 times, sc in next 2 st, *(light peach)* dec, sc in next 2 st, dec, *(pink)* (sc in next 2 st, dec) repeat 2 times [18]
Continue working in pink yarn.
Rnd 19: (sc in next st, dec) repeat 6 times [12]
Stuff the head firmly with fiberfill.
Rnd 20: BLO dec 6 times [6]
Fasten off, leaving a yarn tail. Using your yarn needle, weave the yarn tail through the front loop of each remaining stitch and pull it tight to close. Weave in the yarn end 12.

BODY AND STEM

start in light peach yarn

Pull up a loop of light peach yarn in the second front loop left on round 19 of the head 13. Work the first stitch in the same stitch where you attached the yarn.
Rnd 20: ch 1, FLO (sc in next st, inc in next st) repeat 6 times [18]

16
17
18
19
20
21
22
23
24
25
26
27
28
29
30

Change to green yarn.
Rnd 21 – 24: sc in all 18 st [18]
Rnd 25a: FLO (ch 5, slst in next st) repeat 18 times [18]
Fasten off and weave in the yarn end 14.
The remaining back loops of round 24 will be used to join the petal skirt with the body 15.
Flip the skirt so the pink petals face outward. Insert the body, aligning the last round of the body with the last round of the skirt 16.
Pull up a loop of green yarn in the marked stitch of the skirt and the first leftover back loop of round 24 of the body at once 17.
Note: *The petals should open at the front, as shown in 18. If the position of yours looks different, fix it by twisting the body or moving the starting stitch a little.*
Rnd 25b: ch 1, working through both layers of skirt and back loops of Rnd 24, sc in all 18 st [18]
Rnd 26: BLO sc in all 18 st [18]
Stuff the body firmly with fiberfill and continue stuffing as you go.
Rnd 27: (sc in next 4 st, dec) repeat 3 times [15]
Rnd 28: (sc in next 3 st, dec) repeat 3 times [12]
Rnd 29: (sc in next 2 st, dec) repeat 3 times [9]
Rnd 30 – 41: sc in all 9 st [9]
Stuff the stem firmly with fiberfill.
Rnd 42: (sc in next st, dec) repeat 3 times [6]
Fasten off. leaving a yarn tail.
Optional: *To make the stem sturdier and bendable, you can insert wire into it. Take a piece of wire and bend one end into an eyelet. Cut the wire to the length of the stem + 1 cm. Wrap the bent end with yarn, then carefully insert the wire into the stem* 19.
Using your yarn needle, weave the yarn tail through the front loop of each remaining stitch and pull it tight to close. Weave in the yarn end.

Hold the flower upside down. Pull up a loop of green yarn in the first front loop left on round 25b of the body 20.
Rnd 26: ch 1. FLO sc in all 18 st [18] 21
Slst in first st. Fasten off and weave in the yarn end.

LEAF

→ *make 2, in green yarn*

Ch 13. Stitches are worked around both sides of the foundation chain.
Rnd 1: start in second chain from hook, sc in next 3 ch, hdc in next 3 ch, dc in next 3 ch, hdc in next 2 ch, inc + ch-2-picot + inc in last ch. Continue on the other side of the foundation chain, hdc in next 2 ch, dc in next 3 ch, hdc in next 3 ch, sc in next 3 ch [27]
Fasten off, leaving a long tail for sewing 22.

ARM

→ *make 2, in light peach yarn*

Rnd 1: start 5 sc in a magic ring [5]
Rnd 2 – 10: sc in all 5 st [5]
Fasten off, leaving a long tail for sewing. The arms don't need to be stuffed.

WING 23

→ *make 2, in pale blue yarn*

Ch 7. Crochet in rows.
Row 1: start in fourth ch from hook, 2 tr + dc in this ch, hdc in next ch, sc in next ch, slst in next ch, ch 1, turn [6]
Row 2: skip 1 st, slst in next 2 st, ch 5, turn [2]
Row 3: start in second ch from hook, hdc inc in this ch, hdc in next 2 ch, sc in next ch, sc in next st, ch 1, turn [6]
Leave the remaining stitch unworked.
Row 4: skip 1 st, sc in next 2 st, hdc in next st, hdc inc in next st, hdc in next st, ch 1, turn [6]
Row 5: hdc in next st, hdc inc in next 2 st, inc in next st,

sc in next 2 st [9] 24
Sc in ch-space of row 4 25, inc in unworked stitch of row 2 26. Fasten off, leaving a long tail for sewing 27 28.

ASSEMBLY

- Flatten the arms and sew them to the body, between rounds 20-21 29.
- Sew the wings at the back of the body, 2 stitches apart 30.
- Sew the leaves between rounds 41-42 and rounds 39-40 of the stem.

EMBROIDERY ON FACE

- Embroider bangs on the face between rounds 9-11, using pink yarn.
- Embroider eyes over round 13, 3 stitches apart, using black yarn.
- Split your black yarn in strands and use a single strand to embroider eyelashes on round 13.
- Split your pink yarn in strands and use a single strand to embroider a smile on round 15.
- Embroider rosy cheeks between rounds 14-15, 1 stitch wide, using light pink yarn.